T0147000

GOD'S UNREASONABLE REASONING

What God Is Up To When Things
in Life Don't Make Sense

DR. PRESTON WILLIAMS II

GOD'S UNREASONABLE REASONING
WHAT GOD IS UP TO WHEN THINGS IN LIFE DON'T MAKE SENSE

iUniverse books may be ordered through booksellers or by contacting:

iUniverse
1663 Liberty Drive
Bloomington, IN 47403
www.iuniverse.com
1-800-Authors (1-800-288-4677)

Because of the dynamic nature of the Internet, any web addresses or links contained in this book may have changed since publication and may no longer be valid. The views expressed in this work are solely those of the author and do not necessarily reflect the views of the publisher, and the publisher hereby disclaims any responsibility for them.

Any people depicted in stock imagery provided by Getty Images are models, and such images are being used for illustrative purposes only.
Certain stock imagery © Getty Images.

Scriptures marked KJV are taken from the KING JAMES VERSION (KJV): KING JAMES VERSION, public domain.

Scripture taken from the New King James Version®. Copyright © 1982 by Thomas Nelson. Used by permission. All rights reserved.

ISBN: 978-1-5320-5811-0 (sc)
ISBN: 978-1-5320-5810-3 (e)

Library of Congress Control Number: 2018911697

Print information available on the last page.

iUniverse rev. date: 09/29/2018

Praise for *God's Unreasonable Reasoning*
An acclaimed book reviewer, CEOs, and university executives
and presidents have written endorsements saying:

"This second Christian self-help book in a series encourages readers
to trust in God's plans instead of impulsively pursuing their own...
The author illustrates his lessons with relatable anecdotes from his
own life... In this book, the author clearly offers his perspective
on how life works—it doesn't bend to human wishes or proceed at
random, he says, but develops according to divine will. Along the
way, he proposes achievable habits that he says will help readers
to know God's plan, including prayer, Bible reading, and pursuing
supportive relationships...Overall...this book offers a well-structured
argument with enough everyday examples to make it feel down-to-
earth, rather than unachievably spiritual. A practical and reassuring
work of popular theology."

— *Kirkus Reviews*

"If you are searching for some direction as to the "WHY" of your life
I suggest you fix a cup of tea, find an easy chair, shut off the phone
and sit down with Dr. Williams new book, God's Unreasonable
Reasoning. You will find words of wisdom that will bring clarification
and comfort to the inquiring mind.

Dr. Williams brings to life a vivid portrait of today's concerns and
relates them to scripture. You will find yourself and your life revealed
in the pages of this book and you will be led to bringing closure to
those situations in your life that remain unfinished."

—*Dr. Louise Morley*
Board of Governors, Ombudsman
former Vice Chancellor for Human Resources
Keiser University

"In his book, *God's Unreasonable Reasoning*, Dr Williams skillfully
reminds us that "His ways are not our ways nor His thoughts ours." A
liberating truth we deprive ourselves of when attempting to solve our

challenges, conflicts and disappointments through our own human reasoning. Through his poignant yet unique poetic writing style we relearn old truths and principles reframed in a contemporary vocabulary that bring new insights and yes, new revelation. The more you read, the more you will realize that God's reasoning is not unreasonable after all.

Dr. Williams has given us a new paradigm through which to frame a dynamic and victorious Christian life. The application of the principles in this book will challenge, convict, correct and change you forever!"

—*Dr. Charles Travis*
President & Founder, Aidan University
Presiding Bishop, Logos Global Network of Christian Ministries, Inc.

"This book admirably defends the importance of spiritual intimacy and provides a guide to those who desire a deeper understanding of God's "strategic plan" for their lives through the hills and valleys on the journey through life. Its great insight and wisdom, its extraordinarily lucidity and persuasiveness, come from Dr. Preston William's vast experience in counseling and pastoral leadership and his years of consistent self-discipline through the Word of God. Dr. Williams has produced a work from a posture of sound theological truth yet practical in its realism and relevance."

–– *Dr. Misty Grant*
President, Logos University

"After reading Dr. Williams book *God's Unreasonable Reasoning*, it became quite clear that His reasoning is not unreasonable at all, it is merely how we have taken and distorted it. The three different ways Dr. Williams approaches this complicated subject is the true way we must listen and understand God if we are to change this world by changing ourselves. First, we must know that understanding God will bring about conflict and we are to realize that and overcome those conflicts. Secondly, we must go all the way back to Adam and

Eve and truly understand the relationship we have with God and know that it will not come without trials and tribulations.

And then, we must understand that God's boundaries are there to assist us as we walk hand in hand with Him. Dr. Williams writing style follows his preaching style that is both personal and challenging while also giving us hope for tomorrow. This book is a must read for those who truly want to grow in His grace."

— Dr. Jack Kelly
President, The Opus Group & Business Chaplains International

"It has been stated that people and movements can be defined by the books they read and remember, so it is with great expectation that I introduce Bishop Dr. Preston Williams II "God's Unreasonable Reasoning" to the world. This book is exceptionally well written, inspiring and enlightening as it tackles the paradox of reconciling human logic and God's sovereignty.

Dr. Williams was able to lead his readers to the challenging conclusion that no matter what you are going through, God's will for our lives has reason and purpose. This affirming message of hope and surrendering of our own thoughts and will to trust God's sovereignty is a must read, a discipleship tool and a gem to be treasured. I highly recommend this book to anyone who is willing to discover God's calling to a higher pathway of thinking and living."

— Rev. Dr. N.R. Hyatt
President and CEO
Gateway Church

CONTENTS

DEDICATION

To my lovely bride, my best friend, and Nubian queen—Kathy. Well, here's my book. Nearly everything I have questioned about life and God is in it, and still it is only a glimpse of how God rewrote the text of my life when I opened the book of my heart to His eyes. Thank you for putting up with many late nights and awkward schedules so that the work could be accomplished. You were my second pair of eyes during my writing process. Yours was the understanding and encouragement I greatly needed.

I want to especially thank you for your brilliant cover ideas. It was masterfully designed. I thought nothing could top *The God of How* cover you created in 2013. I was wrong.

Above all, I will be forever grateful to God for joining us as man and wife. Your essence of love is a personal source of inspiration, and a cause for my passionate commitment to excellence in pursuit of knowledge and filling my dreams. It is a privilege to share my ministry, life, and love with you. For that, I lay this book in your proverbial lap, because it's yours. I affectionately dedicate it to you.

FOREWORD

Buckle your seatbelts, this book will take you on one of life's wild rides as you travel through the wilderness of your mind. It revolutionizes the mind and causes you to stop looking and start seeing. Chapter after chapter, Dr. Williams impregnates your mind and penetrates your heart causing construction and destruction to go on simultaneously. You realize that conflict truly is the contractor of your construction team.

This book lowers you into the reality of your own spiritual state and then lifts you into the stark reality of the everlasting love of an Almighty God that works all things for good to them who love Him. You find that God wants us to move from the basement of our minds to the balcony of His mind so that the lens of our lives reflect Him.

God's Unreasonable Reasoning leads us on a journey that substantiates the fact that you can't rationalize God. The more you try to rationalize Him, the more unreasonable God seems. In his book Dr. Williams reveals that when the mind is revolutionized your faith can be resilient and refined. He uses his own valuable life experiences to paint a picture of life's hills and valleys leaving nothing to the imagination. He candidly shares himself so that we may realize that what's powerful and strong in us comes from adversity not advantage. He confirms the fact that you don't know who you really are until you hit rock bottom.

Dr. Williams navigational skills moves you beyond the wrecking ball of life that has paralyzed you with reasoning into the reality that we may never be able to explain Him but will always be able to experience Him. He reveals that freedom comes when relationship is developed through intimacy with the Almighty.

This book is a train of transformation which rides you through life's darkroom where your negatives can be exposed and developed. It opens the eyes of your understanding so that when you reach your final destination you will be able to more clearly comprehend God's unreasonable reasoning.

— Dr. Saundra Gadsden
Supervisor, Pastoral Care
University of Florida Health (UF Health) - Jacksonville

PREFACE

This manuscript is the sequel to my previous book, *The God of How*. In *God's Unreasonable Reasoning*, like *The God of How*, each chapter didn't just happen spontaneously. The insights in each evolved over three decades of research and preparation for lectures, seminars, and sermons. They grew slowly. From the tender roots of experiences planted in the well-prepared soil of life, *God's Unreasonable Reasoning* sprouted, leafed, budded, and blossomed. It has been a very special project brought to fruition through observations, research, and personal experiences. It is a reflection of a few stories from my past and the principles I have learned along my own journey of spiritual growth. I hope they reflect what has happened to all of us at some point in our lives.

In my book *The God of How* I introduced you to God as the Mastermind, Initiator, Source, and Finisher of our lives and to His purpose for giving us life. In this book, it is my intention to mentor you at that point in your life where your past intersects with your present and you are confronted with two important question: Are you willing to discover God's best version of you? Are you open to rethinking your possible future? It is at this point where God's reasoning often intersects with—and seems to conflict with—our reasoning, causing an internal dilemma.

The Bible alludes many times to the difference between what we plan for our life and what God has determined for us in life:

"A man's heart plans his way,
but the Lord directs his steps."

(Proverbs 16:9 NKJV)

"There are many plans in a man's heart,
Nevertheless, the Lord's counsel—that will stand."

(Proverbs 19:21 NKJV)

There is a life apart from what we can see, one that is waiting for us to come into a spiritual place with God to discover it. Joseph Campbell restated Proverbs 19:21 this way: "We must be willing to get rid of the life we have planned so as to have the life that is waiting for us."

If we acknowledge His plans for us and make the right decisions at critical intersections in life, we can expect great things from God through us, by us, and from us. And as a result, our relationship with God will be greatly developed. We will gain a deeper understanding of how critical our daily fellowship with God is, and it will grow immensely. Our relationship will mature to the degree that we will not continue "business as usual" on our previous path—the one without His guidance—but develop and build upon our new path with Him. Our new path will lead to a greater love, higher energy, and surely a greater appreciation, dedication, and commitment to God our Father through his Son, Christ Jesus. May we always be led by the Holy Spirit, open and receptive to the divinity and holiness of God, who is waiting on us at the intersection leading to our new path.

ACKNOWLEDGMENTS

For giving me life so that God can fulfill His purpose apportioned to me, I want to thank my parents, the late Bishop Preston Williams Sr. and my late mother, Pearl Brown Williams. They were precious to me. Thank you for your laughter and your smiles and for providing the love and nurture that was critical for my development from a boy to a man.

I would also like to recognize Dr. N.R. Hyatt CEO and President of Gateway Church, Board Members, Associate Pastors, and my ministry leaders. Thank you for your passionate leadership and spiritual covering. And to all the amazing members and parishioners of Gateway Church in Ft. Lauderdale, FL. Thank you for your thoughts, unfailing support, your tenacity and sensitivity to God's vision and ultimate plan for the amazing future of Gateway Church. Thank you for your service in the Kingdom of God.

I, along with Kathy, feel a deep sense of gratitude to our children and their families: Shantal, Preston III, Jarell Sr., Portia, Sharmayne, and Zaynah. Your love, zest for life, and the pursuit your dreams is an inspiration. Don't ever give up!

To you the reader, the fact that you've chosen this book for your personal library says that you are a visionary who possess the desire and the courage to change. Thank you for making this choice. Finally, to the Source of all we can ask or think, the God of how, the Father and Lord of all creation, and His Son, Jesus Christ, and my personal Counselor, the Holy Spirit. Thank you for the privilege of knowing and serving You.

INTRODUCTION

8. "For My thoughts are not your thoughts,
Nor are your ways My ways," says the Lord.
9. "For as the heavens are higher than the earth,
So are My ways higher than your ways,
And My thoughts than your thoughts.
—Isaiah 55:8-9 (NKJV)

There has always been much conflict concerning God's reasoning and man's human logic. This can be understood within the context of competing worldviews. The dawn of the twenty-first century placed the topic of "worldviews" front and center for discussion and application inside the Christian movement in the United States.

A worldview is the framework from which we view reality, what we use to try to make sense of life and the world. It is any ideology, philosophy, theology, movement, or religion that provides an overarching approach to understanding God, the world, and man's relations to God and the world. Whether conscious or subconscious, every person has some type of worldview. A personal worldview is a combination of all you believe to be true, and it becomes the driving force behind every emotion, decision, and action. Therefore, it affects your response to every area of your life.

Of immediate concern is the worldview clash between two major camps present in the United States today: the biblical worldview and the nonbiblical worldview. In the Genesis experience, before the fall of the human race, there was only one worldview—the Kingdom of

God. Before there was an inspired, canonized book known as the Bible, there was the Kingdom of God.

The opening verse of the Bible sets forth some important facts that are the foundation for the development of a worldview; in this case of course it is the basis for a biblical worldview. Genesis 1:1 says: "In the beginning God created the heaven and the earth." Within this short verse are several profound statements.

First, it states that God created the heaven and the earth. Therefore, He must have existed prior to that creation—and notice, too, that the verse only speaks of one God. Second, the universe had a beginning, and that beginning was created by God. Third, since God created the heaven and the earth, He must be either, or both, superior to and sovereign over His creation. This places God at the center of our preferred belief system. Today, these are the very points that are at the center of conflicts between personal worldviews.

Presenting the "correct" worldview is at the heart of the Bible, from Genesis to Revelation. It is the answer to the question wrapped in the riddle of what seems to be an oxymoron: how to reconcile human logic and God's.

After the fall of man, we see that God made a declaration that revealed a definitive conflict of not only two kingdoms, but also two ideologies. These still impact the world today. God said to the serpent (influenced by the fallen angel Lucifer), "And I will put enmity between you and the woman, And between your seed and her Seed" (Gen. 3:15 NKJV). The seed of the woman represents the Messiah, or His Church—the Kingdom of God. The seed of the serpent represents Lucifer (now known as Satan), who is now the prince of the earth, and his kingdom—the now-fallen world.

God's declaration that the woman's seed will conquer the seed of the serpent was fulfilled in the progressive transition from the Old Testament to the New Testament. Upon the arrival of the Messiah (the seed of the woman), He reintroduced the Kingdom of Heaven. Both Matthew and Luke recorded Jesus's words in the model Lord's Prayer (Matthew 6:9-13; Luke 11:2-4). Both refer to, "Your kingdom come." This translates the Greek text *elthato e basileia sou*. The verb *eltheto* is an ancient Greek imperative, so that the phrase means "let your kingdom come." It is usually assumed that this is a request for God to usher in His kingdom upon earth as promised in scripture. Put another way, the birth of the Messiah was how God ushered in not only a new, "correct" worldview, but a new world order and a transfer of influence and power upon the earth.

So, what exists today is the result of this new world order: a conflict between a biblical worldview (those who believe the Kingdom of Heaven has been reinstated) and a secular humanist worldview (those who believe we're still living in the fallen world). Depending upon which worldview an individual chooses, he or she derives an understanding, interpretation, and response to the world in which he or she lives.

This chosen worldview becomes the basis for answering such questions as:

- Who am I?
- Where did I come from?
- Where am I going?
- Do absolute moral truths exist?
- Is absolute truth defined by the Bible?
- What is true and what is false concerning my experiences?
- How should I conduct my life, or act?
- Is Satan real?
- Does God exist and, if so, what is my response to Him?

In 2005, the Supreme Court handed down its long-awaited decisions on the public display of the Ten Commandments. With the removal of the emblems of the Ten Commandment tablets from our courthouses, schools, etc., "worldview" has become a growing concern in the rapidly changing post-Christian culture. Regardless of the Court's arguments, no serious person can deny that the Ten Commandments are foundational to the Western system of law. The foundation of our legal system was not established in Agnostic atheism, Hinduism, or the writings of Confucius. Modern Western civilization emerged from an explicitly Christian context, and the Ten Commandments—representing the law as handed down by God—were understood to undergird the law as established by men and governments.

And so it is with life. How we govern our life and decisions must be connected with the mind of God. God's word provides the necessary tools critical for our rationale in decision-making. God provides the "map" for us with the Christian Bible. And He provides the "compass" with the Holy Spirit, the One who guides you when you open your heart to His heart, causing the words of the Bible to come alive. Unless God's Spirit applies the Word to your life, the Bible is just another book of literature. These two, the Spirit and the written Word, work together as a Spiritual Navigation System for your life. [1]

This cultural shift away from Christian influence is but one example of the impact of the secular humanist worldview. To understand the secular humanist worldview, we must examine the basic foundation of human reasoning.

So, what is human reasoning in this context? Simply put, it is looking at all human experiences from man's perspective—consciously or unconsciously leaving God out of the process of reasoning. It is trying to figure out spiritual things on our own. It is looking at the challenges of this life with just our physical senses—without acknowledging (by faith) the unseen hand of God providentially orchestrating events for His purpose and our benefit. Human reasoning can even assume that God sees things as we see them.

The common stance of many people today is to build their worldview based on their own theories. Even with members of the Christian faith it is common to hear individuals express, "God doesn't really mean this or that." This type of thinking reflects a belief that humans are capable of reinterpreting the Word of the Bible, making the mandates of God's word of no effect. Satan's method of deception and number one weapon in his arsenal is, "Don't believe anything that can't be supported by human reasoning."

It is a masterpiece of strategic planning. Satan deceives by keeping the minds of men searching and conjecturing about plans that God has not made known, by having us believe we understand the purpose of every challenging experience. God does not actually intend that we should, at first, understand these.

As a Christian, of course you want to make decisions according to God's will. But what happens when you just don't know which way God wants you to go? Sooner or later in life we all must make some critical life decisions. It can be difficult, and many Christians struggle with this—because of the temptation of letting human reasoning override the will of God.

Ultimately, we must come to terms with the fact that God's will for our lives has reason and purpose. To execute God's will, however, we must first know His will. This is only possible through a personal relationship with Him and a proper understanding of His mind, which is recorded for us in the Holy Scriptures. Our human reasoning must be weighed, balanced, and scrutinized as we submit ourselves to the pursuit of a perfect consecration with God and conscientiousness toward God.

> God's reasoning is not unreasonable when we understand His complete uniqueness and sovereignty.

To be clear, the soul must lay down her own will and present herself in humility before God. There must be a great love for God and an earnest desire to know His will. We must acknowledge that we are dependent on Him and that life will be an utter failure unless He wills, guides, plans, and works within us—with us and for us.

God's reasoning will not seem unreasonable if we understand that because of His complete uniqueness and sovereignty, God is able to declare, "Truly I am God, I have no peer; I am God, and there is none like me, who announces the end from the beginning and reveals beforehand what has not yet occurred, who says, 'My plan will be realized; I will accomplish what I desire'" (Isa. 46:9-10 NET Bible; see also Isa. 14:24; 43:13).

Everyone has a grid of reasoning through which we perceive every experience that happens in life. This grid forms the basis for our general belief about what is true. We call these truths our values (good, bad, or indifferent), and they in turn determine how we respond to life.

In many cases, we find our human reasoning in conflict with God's will. But if we submit ourselves to the unknown possibilities of God, at some point, amid all the confusion, conflict, and contemplation, the mysteries of God will breakthrough upon us by the illumination of His word. It is there in the Bible: we must abandon our human rationale to embrace the incomprehensible reasoning of God and relate our experience to His omniscience and omnipotence.

People, even Christians, won't always understand the choices God leads us to make. In fact, it may feel as if sometimes we're making foolish decisions. But God does not require us to understand His reasoning, just to obey it, even if it seems unreasonable.

True obedience to God means doing what He says, when He says it, how He says it should be done, and for the duration of time He says to do it—regardless of whether or not you understand the reasons for it—until He declares that his intent has been accomplished.

Such a resolve requires faith. And although faith is, in part, an act of the intellect, or should I say human reasoning, it is more the act of forcing the intellect to subscribe to a Divine truth influencing movement of the human will, which is itself moved by the grace of God.

My purpose in writing this book is to reinforce that, no matter what you are going through, you should feel comfortable subsuming your own thoughts and will to trust God's "unreasonable" reasoning. To help you reach a mental place where, when you ask God to teach you His will, you will have faith and believe that He will do it. And when God begins to unfold His plan, you will have the courage to move according to His order without doubting or questioning His higher reasoning.

Nothing can compare to discovering and following the Divine plan for your life. So, when God's plan seems challenging in a given situation, just obey God and leave all the consequences to Him—even when His plans seem a little foolish according to human logic.

Author's Note

The English language is blessed with an abundance of fine Bible translations. While most modern English translations are based on careful study of the text in the original languages, it is important to remember the limitations of translations. It is very difficult to capture the full range and depth of meaning intrinsic to a text steeped in a foreign language and culture.

Today we read from a broad cross section of Bible translations. In keeping with our long-established and fluid practice of picking a translation based on the language style or word choice related to a particular passage, I've used a variety of translations in this manuscript, including the King James Version, New International Version, the English Standard Version, the New American Standard Version, the New Living Translation, and others.

The purpose of Bible translation has always been to put it in the language of the common people. You may ask, "What is the best translation of the Bible?" And my reply will be, "The one that is read and obeyed, not the one that is gathering dust on the shelf!"

PART I

UNDERSTANDING GOD AND CONFLICT

CHAPTER 1

HEART-THINKING OR GOD THINKING?

People mistakenly assume that their thinking is done by their head;
it is actually done by the heart which first dictates the conclusion,
then commands the head to provide the reasoning that will defend it.
— Anthony de Mello

WE ALL STARTED BEING INFLUENCED by the world the moment we were conceived in our mother's womb. According to the Bible, we are born into sin. The carnal mind has created intuitive tracks that our mind runs on. As we move through life, we are exposed to a diversity of situations and encounters. Instinctively, our carnal mind knows how we've responded to those experiences in the past and responses accordingly. This confirms the fact that we've been conformed to the image of the world from day one. Consequently, whenever we come up against challenging situations accompanied by temptation, we are inclined to go down that intuitive track our mind runs on again and again, unless, through the Spirit, we are given a new way to think and walk altogether.

Here's one of the strategies the Devil uses for luring people away from God's plan for their lives: deception. He makes people pay dearly for what

> The heart is in a constant two-way dialogue with the mind.

has been freely given to them by God through the blood of Jesus. You are created to be able to operate with a higher-thinking capability, like God. The plan for heaven and earth started in the mind of God before He created them. The bible says, "all things created came out of the unseen" (Heb. 11:3 Aramaic Bible in Plain English). Thoughts exist in the unseen realm and materialize in the physical realm through faith. [1]

If you're not a Christian, or even if you are but you don't yet feel secure in your knowledge of God's ways or in your relationship with Him, you may not be aware of how to walk in the Spirit. Don't worry, just keep reading. It will become clearer to you what that means. Because we are all born unaware of how to walk in the Spirit or how to be spiritually minded, the problem is we only know what we know. All our life we've been carnally minded, so when we come up against a challenging situation, we react to it like we've always reacted. To understand how we relate to life and all its experiences, we must first understand the human mind.

In the study of psychology, the human mind is said to be comprised of three basic spheres and functions: cognition, feelings, and volition. The cognitive sphere of the mind is composed of mental actions we commonly connect with "thinking," such as acquiring knowledge and understanding through thought, experience, and the senses. As a result, a perception, sensation, notion, or intuition is formed and is employed as a significant part of our everyday life in figuring things out.

As it relates to heart-thinking, which I explain in more detail later, the feeling (or emotional) function of the mind is our internal monitor, which reacts to any given situation or set of circumstances. We are emotionally complex human beings who experience a broad range of emotions from happiness to sadness, from enthusiasm to depression, from joy to sorrow, from satisfaction to frustration, and so on. It would be unfair to the cognitive sphere of the mind to assume it functions alone, without the influential culprit we call the heart.

Let's explore the role the heart plays in creating emotional experience and assessing situations without conscientious reasoning, and how this experience can be augmented by the Spirit of God's influence if we give it its proper role in helping us make decisions. The heart is one of the most important components of the human body, because it is one of the main mediums for connecting us to each other and the Universe. The commonly accepted definition of the heart is not complete. In addition to being an organ that pumps blood, the heart also has an intelligence of its own. It has been characterized by some neurologists as our second brain, or mind.

The heart is in a constant two-way dialogue with the mind. It is through this dynamic communication process that the consciousness of the heart can change how the mind processes information. Our emotions are transmitted far more quickly and often to the cognitive mind by way of the heart and the intuitive tracks developed from birth than the mind can send them to the heart. This plays a direct and important role in determining our perceptions, thought processes, and emotional experiences.

Which brings us to the third sphere and function of the mind: volition. The first two spheres and functions of the mind, cognition and feelings, contribute to the formation of our volition, or will. The "will" is our ultimate driving force. Within this sphere of the mind lie our agendas, purposes, goals, values, desires, drives, motivations, and commitments. This is the mind's engine, which accelerates us up and moves us forward, slows us down, or backs us away from a situation, action, or choice.

Despite the reality that cognition (informed thoughts), feeling (heart), and volition (will) are equally important functions of the mind, it is cognition, or thinking, that is instrumental to grasping the other two. Herein lies the importance of the "transformation of the mind" reflected in the book of Romans, chapter twelve. If we want to change a feeling, we must identify the thinking that ultimately led us to that feeling. If we want to change a desire, again it is the thinking that informs the drive that must be identified and adjusted if our behavior and choices in life are to be altered successfully.

Consider this example. You're torn between two options—one risky, the other safe. The risky option is a quick business, financial, or relationship decision. Even though you know it's more than you can or should handle, time is running out. You are influenced by those close to you, and the popular mixed opinions of media sources are complicating the issue. You're not sure exactly whether the decision you are leaning toward will fit into your current and immediate need, but you are convinced you need to act now. Your heart is shouting a clear "yes," telling you how great you will feel with this issue behind you. Shouting "yes" just as loudly, however, is your head and its human reasoning, which provides historical information from past experiences to defend your heart's need to make an emotional decision.

Your God-regenerated spirit is clamoring for your attention, encouraging you to obey God's word concerning the choice. But the heart and mind keep questioning that pull to do what is safe, tempting you to contradict God's counsel. At some level, you recognize that you should give yourself permission to plunge into His will, thereby avoiding a possibly disastrous situation. The problem is that we aren't always sure if we're correctly hearing God's voice. Additionally, sometimes what we think is God's voice is really our voice, the voices of other people we've deemed credible influences in our life, or even worse, the voice of the enemy.

Sometimes, even well-meaning friends and family will encourage you to "listen to your heart," telling you it "knows what's best for you." But is that good advice when your heart is not submitted to the counsel of the Spirit of God? In retrospect, think back on some instances when you did follow your heart blindly. How did it work out for you? Maybe there were occasions when you threw caution to the wind and let your emotions take the wheel, and all went well. But it's likely there are at least as many times when your decision delivered the opposite outcome.

Unfortunately, we tend to be bad at analyzing statistics when it comes to calculating the successes and failures of our own prior experiences. For most people, traumatic memories tend to fade with time, but we still keep them in our mental arsenal and remember them when it comes time to weigh the risk of new experiences that challenge our comfort zones. As a result, we're almost programmed to go with our heart, because we remember the lingering scars of bad decisions or borderline successes. Our heart is great at providing the guidance in the moment, to help us gain immediate relief. But too often we forget the long-term effects of following it.

Heart-thinking has its genesis in the realm of emotions. As human beings, we have certain proclivities. For one, we tend to respond to life's challenging experiences with a basic instinctive need to survive. Without the benefit of God's reasoning, we depend upon emotions and cognitive biases partly so that we can make quick judgments. These might not always be the "best" resolutions to a problem, but we often think of them as "sufficient" because they help us err on the side of survival. It is an experimental process liable to failure. Emotions are not God's word, so stop listening to them like they are.

Your emotions and instinctive bodily feelings are not designed to carry the burden of proof you put upon them. Emotions were never intended to be and *are still not* infallible guidance systems. They only employ shallow rationale, only provide immediate relief.

Time passes, life happens, and we continue to experience bodily and mental feelings as we experience day-to-day challenges or think about past events. We marry the love of our life, everyone celebrates, we get a job promotion, we get feelings we come to label as "good" or "positive." We also get feelings that are not so pleasant, which we often label as "bad" or "negative."

These are merely mental classifications that we employ to categorize our experiences, and we then respond to those as if they are real. In fact, they exist only in our body and mind until our emotions drive us to act. The truth is that a complex, intricate relationship exists between thinking and emotions. For every thought we have, we generate a reciprocal feeling, which I have chosen to classify as "heart-thinking."

Simply put, heart-thinking is when an individual experience the inability to recognize strong emotions as merely emotions. These tend to interfere with decisions we would otherwise make with informed thoughts (either spiritual, academic, and/or experiential knowledge), resulting in distorted views of situations and relationships. Individuals who rely on heart-thinking are likely to conclude that their emotional reactions prove that something is true, regardless of evidence to the contrary.

Now let us consider how emotions fit into this heart-thinking component. The study of psychology endorses the fact that emotions are created in the psychological-physiological space between the way we think about the world and our actual experience of it. When we get what we expect, we tend to feel the more pleasant emotions. When we get less than we expect or something different and unwanted, we experience the negative emotions.

The mental pathway of least resistance, what psychologists often refer to as the "default mode" of human thought, is to go with our "gut feelings" or "heart-thinking." This can be adaptive. If we experience something extraordinarily unpleasant or offensive, we have an emotional disgust response and try to avoid it. Future encounters with the same unpleasant thing will therefore not need a second assessment to determine a course of action—we will simply just feel anger, disgust, fear, or regret, and try to avoid it again.

From the book of Exodus to the book of Judges, the story is told of the nation of Israel and its obsession with heart-thinking. This led to a cycle of sin, judgment, and deliverance. God was continually attempting to develop Israel's spiritual IQ. But instead of committing themselves to God and His laws, the Israelites were committed to their heart-thinking.

The stories recorded in the book of Judges reveal God's people following a pattern: Israel turns from God, God turns Israel over to the oppressive surrounding nation, Israel then turns back to God and cries out for help. God then raises up a judge to deliver them.

Israel is repeatedly seen as wavering in faith, worshipping idols, indulging in violence, and generally becoming just like the other nations around it. But they had a special mission: they were chosen to represent God to those other people. Fast-forward to the twenty-first century. Israel's experiences represent the cycle we all go through with God when we give in to heart-thinking: we rebel against God's will, God disciplines us, we repent, and God delivers us. Once in the comfortable position of having been delivered, we give right back in to our heart-thinking ways, starting the cycle over again. Until we are transformed by renewing our minds and bringing our emotions under control—by subjecting them to God's truth—this vicious cycle continues.

Heart-thinking only tells us about ourselves and reinforces what we already think. It is a primitive feedback mechanism, one we evolved to help us believe the prejudice of our current thinking in any fight-or-flight situation is correct. Notice what the Apostle Paul says to the church at Corinth concerning the "spirit" of a man: "For what man knows the things of a man except the spirit of the man which is in him?" (1 Corinthians 2:11 NKJV). He could be defining heart-thinking here. When the spirit of a man is in direct conflict with the Spirit of God, we come face-to-face with an ultimatum influenced by what the Apostle Paul identifies as "strongholds."

Spiritual strongholds are designed to choke out every good thing in your life. Paul pens a second letter to the church of Corinth and interprets the metaphor. He mandates that they destroy the strongholds at their roots before it destroys them: "We demolish arguments and every pretension that sets itself up against the knowledge of God, and we take captive every thought to make it obedient to Christ" (2 Corinthians 10:5 NIV). The "arguments" are the philosophies, reasoning, and schemes of secular worldviews. These pretensions are related to anything man-centered.

> The more dominant the emotional mind becomes, the more it renders the Word of God ineffective.

If we elevate heart-thinking to a reliable mechanism for decision-making, we are setting ourselves up for trouble. Emotions essentially exist as echoes of our thoughts manifested in the body, and they reflect our current thinking. In the book of Jeremiah, we are given a glimpse into the mystery of heart-thinking. The prophet says this about God's view on the matter: "The heart is deceitful above all things, and desperately sick; who can understand it? I the LORD search the heart and test the mind" (Jeremiah 17:9-10

ESV). Therein lies the castle of passion, with fortresses defended by lust, pleasure, and greed. And there is the pinnacle of pride, where the human heart sits enthroned and revels in thoughts of its own excellence and sufficiency. This struggle between self-centeredness and God's desire for our life is an invisible battle that goes on in all our minds, every day.

In the spiritual realm of God, heart-thinking is a major component in what is known in the Christian arena as "the battle of the mind." The mind is where the battle begins, because it is the member of the body that influences consensus and conformity. The battle of the mind exists on many levels, setting people up against the knowledge and will of God. When our minds are not aligned with God's truth and His will, our thoughts are driven by our emotions. Emotional mistakes are often the result of acting on feelings prior to acting on thoughts. This is the reason why the Lord searches the heart and tests the mind. God understands His own creation and knows that what the heart feels can, and often does, come before rational thought. The emotional mind is far quicker than the rational mind, hence provoking heart-thinking. We often spring into action without pausing to consider what we are doing.

The more intense the feeling, the more dominant the emotional mind becomes, and the more likely it is the word of God will be rendered ineffectual. This exposes us to vulnerable tendencies and self-centeredness. With such self-centeredness, and resistance to God's counsel, how can heart-thinking (however strong and labelled as "right") evaluate the quality of a decision? How can it compare options, decide the worth of criteria? How can it reason, eliminate, take different perspectives, etc.? Heart-thinking is not designed to do that. It's a symptom of a cause: the energy in motion, that is, "e-motion" in your body proceeding from the thoughts you already have. Primarily using your heart-thinking as your "yes" or "no" indicators cannot give you the same quality decision that God's counsel can.

The apostle Paul confirms this when he writes to the church of Rome saying:

"And do not be conformed to this world, but be transformed by the renewing of your mind, that you may prove what is that good and acceptable and perfect will of God."

(Romans 12:2 NKJV)

Additionally, he writes to admonish the church at Corinth. Paul rejected worldly wisdom, and in place of it advocated the standard of God's wisdom. He challenged Christians to embrace this standard and to *critically examine all things*:

"For who knows a person's thoughts except the spirit of that person, which is in him? So also no one comprehends the thoughts of God except the Spirit of God. Now we have received not the spirit of the world, but the Spirit who is from God, that we might understand the things freely given us by God. And we impart this in words not taught by human wisdom but taught by the Spirit, interpreting spiritual truths to those who are spiritual. The natural person does not accept the things of the Spirit of God, for they are folly to him, and he is not able to understand them because they are spiritually discerned. [15] The spiritual person judges all things, but is himself to be judged by no one. [16] For who has understood the mind of the Lord so as to instruct him? But we have the mind of Christ."

(1 Corinthians 2:11-16 ESV)

Despite the failures inherent in man's reasoning processes, God still expects us to pursue biblical truth through critical thinking guided by the word of God. Many Christians hesitate at the discussion of critical thinking. They associate the phrase with skepticism and criticism of the Bible and religion. "Critical" in the biblical sense of the word, however, comes from the common Greek words *krites*, which means "to judge" and *kritikos* meaning "able to judge (or discern)." This is the root of the English word "critical."

The word "*kritikos*" appears only once in the New Testament but is attributed to the Word of God: "For the word of God is living and active and sharper than any two-edged sword, and piercing as far as the division of soul and spirit, of both joints and marrow, and able to judge (kritikos) the thoughts and intentions of the heart" (Hebrews 4:12 ESV). Therefore, logic and reasoning that remains faithful to the Bible can accurately be considered "critical thinking." As we explore legitimate authority of influence in the battle for the mind, let us not forget that only reasoning that begins with God constitutes good judgment.

So, where did this battle of the mind begin? The narrative of the entire Bible explores the spiritual conflict that exists between God and Satan that began in heaven and is perpetual in our world even today. Consequently, this conflict involves you and I (mankind). In the beginning of the Bible narrative, God created Adam and Eve, not with the evil nature we see displayed in all of mankind, but with His divine nature. God pronounced their nature, or their heart, as "very good." He purposefully allowed them to be exposed to and tested by Satan, who introduces the couple to a different set of beliefs, attitudes, purposes, and character than God.

As this narrative continues, we discover that, without heeding the counsel of God, they freely made the choice to embrace the evil influence of Satan. That one decision outside of God's influence initiated the corruption of mankind's heart. This event set in motion the dominion of fallen nature and heart-thinking over heeding God's word.

In this, we also realize that a spirit being can communicate with a human by transferring thoughts. Unfortunately, we usually assume that *we* have generated these thoughts ourselves—we often don't recognize Divine influence when it happens. Hence, spiritual conflict now extends to mankind. This change of character from the way God created us, reinforces the degenerative process; this extends past personal corruption to the present conflict and corruption of this entire present world.

In Christendom, we refer to this conflict as "spiritual warfare." Spiritual warfare is the declared posture in which the Christian takes a stand against ungodly influences that are capable of intervening in human affairs. Consequently, when someone on earth tries to bring the influence of the kingdom of God to earth, Satan flares up against them with three of his most effective and intimidating weapons: pride, fear, and, anger. This is why it seems as though a person following the will of God will sometimes have the most difficult tests, trials, and resistance (as opposed to some saints, who are casual seekers of God).

It is important to note that Satan hates God. He is not particularly interested in you as an individual, he is interested in disturbing the plans and purposes God intended for your life, because these will bring God praise, honor, and renown as the one Supreme Being, creator, and ruler of the universe. You and I are incidental to this spiritual conflict. God has decreed this conflict between Him and Satan will be dealt with in the dimension of mankind, which is why we are involved. Make no mistake about it, the bigger war is not ours, but every battle in the war is ours to fight. These battles begin in the mind. It is intense. It is sometimes relentless, and it is unfair because Satan never plays fair. And the reason why it is so intense is that Satan wants to maintain control of your greatest asset—your mind.

To dominate in this battle, we must understand that although the mind is the center of attack, the heart is the arsenal of passion and belief. We must first choose to adjust our thought-life and submit our minds to the Spirit of God by adhering to His word (as laid out in the Bible) if we are to expect authentic transformation in our life. When we do this, God will then change our hearts to embrace His counsel, despite how unreasonable it may seem. Then we have the option to be spiritually minded. God can renew your mind and rewrite what you do and how you think when your intuitive tracks want to guide you in the carnal direction of heart-thinking.

The ultimatum in every decision that you will ever make can be summed up in the words of Joshua to the next generation of Israelites:

"Now therefore fear the Lord and serve him in sincerity and faithfulness. Put away the gods that your fathers served beyond the River and in Egypt, and serve the Lord. And if it is evil in your eyes to serve the Lord, choose this day whom you will serve, whether the gods your fathers served in the region beyond the River, or the gods of the Amorites in whose land you dwell. But as for me and my house, we will serve the Lord."

(Joshua 24:14-15 ESV)

In the lives of believers, challenges, hardships, and temptations can become overwhelming, which can rob the believer of enthusiasm for trusting God, cause them to give in to their own fallible understanding, and make decisions based on heart-thinking. The results can be catastrophic. Each one of us is given a choice. We can choose to think with our heart, or we can choose to submit our thinking to the counsel of God. It is the most important decision you will ever make.

The heart-thinking Christian goes where he or she wants to go and does what he or she wants to do. The spiritually mature Christian goes where God wants him or her to go. His thoughts are accomplished in ways that surpass any and all expectations we can ever have. God's thoughts, plans, ways, methods, and strategies are infinitely higher and greater than our own. If left to our human reasoning, we will fail to fully walk in the full counsel of God, which will lead to poor decisions.

The goal of all believers should be to avoid being deceived by our own understanding and to develop a listening ear that hears the voice of God with confidence. Our goal is to have such intimacy with God that we can walk in the full blessing of our decisions and to be assured they are not based on our own reasoning alone. This does *not* mean that we shouldn't use the intellectual and logical skills that He *has* equipped us with, however.

It is important that we gather all the information and facts involved in making a decision, and then weigh them against God's counsel, pray over them in His presence, and trust the Holy Spirit to sway our mind in the direction of God's will. God, in most cases, will guide us by presenting His reasoning to our mind. This enables us to make decisions and respond to situations in a righteous way, for righteous results.

So, when you are faced with some of life's challenging situations and you must make major decisions, you can either resort to figuring things out with heart-thinking, or by relying on a close relationship with God. If you take the time and put in the effort to develop that relationship, it will help your understanding of His will. To choose the latter would mean that you will not continue "business as usual," but develop and build upon your interaction with God so that there will be nothing hindering you from hearing His voice.

> God still expects us to pursue biblical truth through Godly critical thinking.

To conclude, there is a point in all our lives where our past experiences will intersect with our present experiences and we will be confronted with making important decisions. Two of the most valuable scriptural reflections I want to leave you with to sum up this chapter are found in the book of Proverbs. The Bible alludes to the fact that there is a difference between what we think and plan for our life, and what God has determined for us in life:

"A man's heart plans his way,
But the Lord directs his steps."
(Proverbs 16:9 NKJV)

"There are many plans in a man's heart,
Nevertheless, the Lord's counsel—that will stand."
(Proverbs 19:21 NKJV)

CHAPTER 2

CONFRONTATIONS

Difficulties are meant to rouse, not discourage.
The human spirit is to grow strong by conflict.
–William Ellery Channing

MOST PEOPLE DON'T LIKE CONFLICT or confrontation. If you do, you are in the minority. Many people are petrified of it, and will do most anything to avoid conflict. So, when faced with a difficult situation or person, they either evade it or him/her as long as possible, or react prematurely. People respond this way in all kinds of situations: when encountering something new or with change in general, when forced to examine their past failures or their present responsibilities, and even when looking at future dreams that they feel like they'll never achieve because of current hardships. But the problem with not dealing well with the things in life that confront us is that you stay stuck. You don't make any progress.

Conflict and confrontation happen. There's no avoiding them. When conflict comes up, you have to deal with it head-on. Don't let it fester. It's a big mistake to think, "I'll ignore it and hope it will go away." I must ask you to think about this question: Do you believe God can guide you in conflict and confrontation, even if you feel fear or intimidation? In God's infinite wisdom, conflict and confrontation go hand in hand. To better understand confrontation, it is important to note that the English word "confront" originated from a compound

Latin word, *con*, meaning *together* and *frontis*, meaning *front*. "Confront" means *front to front*, or *face-to-face*. It is God's designed strategy that we confront, come face-to-face, with our problems "together" with Him for purposeful correction. Our most compelling emblem of not shying away from conflict, but turning to take it head-on, is the "originator and perfecter of our faith, who for the joy that was set before Him endured the cross, despising the shame" (Hebrews 12:2 NKJV).

> Your relationship with God is dependent upon your obedience to Him.

One reason that avoiding conflict we find ourselves in is not wise and poses a problem is because problems often worsen with negligence. But another reason is that it cuts us off from the most significant opportunities for grace and growth. God does his deepest work in our lives by helping guide us through difficult decisions. Not when all seems right with the world, not when times are easy. It's during the toughest times, the hardest conversations, and the most painful relational tensions that the light of His grace shines brightest and transforms us. There are a plethora of issues in our society today, but the challenge of working out the Christian life in a non-Christian culture is one of the most pressing. This requires divine navigation. We have so many paths we could take in life, but following God's path is the only way to stay on course with His destiny for your life.

If you have any experience boating, you know how essential it is to stay on course. If you steer just a few degrees off the desired course, you can wind up far from where you wanted to go. A slight deviation, if left uncorrected, can result in great devastation. It is the same spiritually. Among God's many diverse methods and means, conflict and confrontation are among His most effective tools for spiritual correction in life. Make no mistake about it: going through a correction is not a nicety. It is, however, a necessity. If our lives veer off course and continue in that wrong direction, it can result in the shipwreck of our faith and our preordained destiny. Because of that fact, God not only designs purposeful conflict, but He desires to confront you with it as a means of correction.

It is essential to experience times of conflict, but never easy. A poignant question was posed to me during a counseling session not too long ago. The question was: "Where is God in my darkest situations, when I need Him the most and can't sense His presence or His will?" I thought of that question as I was researching this chapter on confrontation. It is really the foundational question beneath all of our other questions about life. Most of us are yearning to know God's mind concerning our needs, our frustrations, our problems, and our unclear future paths. We have a deep desire to know His perspective, wisdom, and guidance when we are confronted with life's most difficult challenges. Psalm 43:3, includes the phrase "send out Your light and Your truth! Let them lead me." Here's a promise: God's light (His presence in your life) and God's truth (the accuracy of His word) will lead you, *if* you will allow them to guide you.

You cannot receive heavenly navigation from a distance. Receiving direction from God is a very personal thing. In order for something to be personal, you must of course have a connection to it, or a relationship with it. Your relationship with God is dependent upon your obedience to Him. Have you ever realized how easily we can forget that God causes our destinies to become clear? Yet we choose not to commune with Him until we are in need. In any relationship, lack of communication can cause misunderstandings, resentments, and feelings that you are emotionally far away or distant from each other. This is what happens when you refuse to listen to and obey God, and choose to distance yourself from Him. When you are in a dark moment of life, facing conflict, it's easy to begin thinking all the wrong thoughts. Thoughts like, "Has God forgotten me? Has He given up on me? Is there something wrong with me? Why has He taken away His blessing on my life? Am I no longer of any value to Him? Does He just not care about me anymore?" Guess what? None of those things are true. When you feel any of those things, it's likely because of an overlooked problem with your personal relationship with God.

The problem many people have is that, when God *does* speak, He shares a lot more than we really want to hear or are prepared to follow. God, in His love and mercy, often confronts us with things that we need to change inside us, in our relationship with Him, and in our relationships with other people. But let's be honest; the Bible presents some difficult counsel and principles. If we were given the choice, we would cut out or, as one scripture refers to it, "taking away from of it" the scriptures we deemed unreasonable or not relevant.

I recall reading an article about President Thomas Jefferson, whose religious beliefs were described as a complex issue. In 1803, he pieced together a short comparison of various religions and philosophies, including Christianity. The article revealed that President Jefferson made a little book of his own by taking scissors and cutting out the parts of the Bible that he liked—extracting only what he believed to be the real teachings of Jesus, and arranged them on the pages of a blank book, in a certain order of time or subject! The work is commonly referred to as the "Jefferson Bible."[1]

While I don't believe any of us would be so brazen as to do such a thing, in effect we often do. We don't literally cut out the difficult parts, but we ignore them or don't work at understanding them, and we balk at submitting to those parts when faced with conflicts and the confrontation and correction of God!

Pride is at the heart of all disobedience to God—and almost all form of conflicts. If God opposes the proud but gives grace to the humble (James 4:6), then you want to make sure you're not making yourself God's opponent! As God confronts us with His truth about our lives—as He will if we allow Him—He is also able to provide us with the power we need to respond appropriately.

It is important to understand that when God chose us, He also infused us with His Spirit, giving us the ability to grow in spiritual maturity. Yes, it is true that God loves us just the way we are, but He will never leave us just the way we are. It is historically proven that our growth in God takes place through pivotal, life-changing experiences that He not only allows to happen, but, in some instances, orchestrates Himself. Through these confrontations He challenges our hypocrisy, He questions the sincerity of our love toward Him, He judges our willingness to substitute other authorities in His place, and He reveals our lust for worldly success over His Kingdom's priority and progress.

God approaches His relationship with us like this because of His love for us. Out of His love for us, God will challenge sin in our lives wherever He finds it. Why? Because God won't tolerate being second place in our lives. We are His people, and He will not become just one of many gods of our own making. He demands to be the sovereign over everything in our lives, not just a source of strength for us to use to accomplish our own purposes. There is an old saying that goes, "He must be the Lord *of* all, or he won't be the Lord *at* all."

Through life's many conflicts, God challenges us to commit to a deeper holiness, to a greater faithfulness, and to living a pure life. He is always renewing us as His people, both as individuals and as a church body. Many people I've met through almost forty years of ministry have literally referred to certain misfortunes in their lives as unreasonable on God's part. They believe that there was a better way God could have handled a situation or even communicated His will regarding a set of circumstances. When God's reasoning seems unreasonable to us, we must take a look at ourselves and the root of such thinking.

It begins with the pride of refusing to accept our own level of spiritual immaturity. We insulate ourselves against admitting our own spiritual needs, then tell ourselves that we don't have anything to adjust or improve in our relationship with God. Usually we try to justify the way we handled situations that led to failure, or we blame other people

> God's "unreasonable" reasoning is calling us to a higher way.

or circumstances for undesirable outcomes. We even attempt cover up our inadequacy by trying harder to accomplish things our way, without the benefit of God's counsel. Finally, we become desensitized to God's Spirit. The frightening thing about being desensitized to God's Spirit is that it leads to a lack of desire to respond to the person that God is calling us to be, to the purpose He has predestined for us. This causes God great pain, because He sacrificed so much for us, loves us so much, and has invested so much in us.

But would God ever give up on us? No. No matter how great the drift or how wide the divide, our hope really is in God's faithfulness to us. I have come to the total conviction that nothing shall separate us from the love of God through Christ Jesus. In Apostle Paul's writing to the Christian church in Rome (Romans 8:35-39), he strongly expresses his disavowal of the possibility of some secret force one day erupting into our lives and resulting in the love of Christ being torn away from us. No such potency exists—not on earth, not in hell, and not in heaven. There is nothing whatsoever that can separate God's people from God's love. No one and nothing can do this.

Paul goes on to list the common troubles and conflicts that Christians meet, and he challenges them one by one. He challenges them by saying:

> "Who shall separate us from the love of Christ? Shall trouble, or hardship, or persecution, or famine, or nakedness, or danger, or sword? As it is written: "For your sake we face death all day long; we are considered as sheep to be slaughtered." No, in all these things we are more than conquerors through Him who loved us. For I am convinced that neither death nor life, neither angels nor demons, neither the present nor the future, nor any powers, neither height nor depth, nor anything else in all creation, will be able to separate us from the love of God that is in Christ Jesus our Lord."
>
> (Romans 8:35-39 NIV)

As you can see, the heart of much human conflict and confrontation stems not from God abandoning us, but from our disconnecting from Him. This leads to the conviction that it is up to *us* to make our own way and create our own solutions and execute our own justice. By rejecting God's love and guidance and trying to live our own way, we in effect try to become our own gods. The problem with this type of self-driven posturing happens when we begin dealing with the fiery darts of conflict in the natural realm. We are not fighting the good fight of faith, but rather we're fighting the fight of flesh. By doing so, we become more and more fragmented as we try to establish our own fallible view of right and wrong and defend our inadequate responses to conflict in this world.

Conflict and confrontation in relationships are especially difficult to navigate, particularly through a lens of God's strategic spiritual plan. Many of us do this poorly or not at all. We tend to default toward one of two paths: either we find ourselves confronting everything, or we run from conflict. This is referred to as "fight or flight." It doesn't take too long to realize that *both* of these methods are, more often than not, ineffective. Jesus was never afraid to confront, but his confrontation was strategic and specific rather than generalized or nebulous.

There are those of us who are genuinely striving as hard as we can to live a righteous Christian life, and we try to apply that to everyone God allows us to intersect with. Even those people—perhaps *especially* those—can still make fools of themselves by falling into the ever-present trap of responding to someone in a very wrong way. It's easy to cause offense by behaving or speaking in an obnoxious, un-Christian manner. When this happens, God's strategy concerning conflict in relationships often begins to strike us as unreasonable, because we feel embarrassed. Christ commanded us to repent, *truly* repent, just as Christ also commanded us to forgive, *truly* forgive, the repentant. We must forgive others if God is going to forgive us. Notice what we are challenged to personify:

> "For if ye forgive men their trespasses, your heavenly Father will also forgive you: but if ye forgive not men their trespasses, neither will your Father forgive your trespasses."
>
> (Matthew 6:14-15 KJV)

"Then came Peter to him, and said, Lord, how oft shall my brother sin against me, and I forgive him? till seven times? Jesus saith unto him, I say not unto thee, Until seven times: but, Until seventy times seven."

(Matthew 18:21-22 KJV)

The goal of confrontation in relationships should always be restoration. While it is easy to internalize our hurt and pack our feelings down deep inside, or to gossip about others to make ourselves feel better about ourselves, this is not God's reasoning, it is the reasoning of fallen mankind. The temptation is to confront someone so we can vent our feelings or to hurt someone who has hurt us. So, although God tell us to respond in love, our initial internal emotional thought is often: "That's not going to happen—it's unreasonable to think I should be nice to the person who offended me or hurt me deeply." Believe it or not, love is the driving force behind all of God's reasoning. The goal in confrontation should be to restore your relationship with the other person—and their relationship with God too. "One way the enemy keeps a person in an offended state is to keep the offense hidden, cloaked with pride. Pride will keep you from admitting your true condition . . . Pride causes you to view yourself as a victim. Your attitude becomes, 'I was mistreated and misjudged; therefore, I am justified in my behavior.'"[2]

> Beware of your cycles of self-torture.

In a world filled with antagonists, people who are self-aggrandized, and even opportunists, being a people-judger or a people-pleaser is quick, easy, and one of the most unloving things you can do. God's unreasonable reasoning calls us to a higher way. We are meant to forgive and, with Christian confrontation, lovingly address serious sin. It goes without saying that conflict can cause anger, hurt, confusion, fear, and damaged relationships. At the same time, if approached in a God-honoring way, conflict can bring stimulation, healing, resolution to problems, and strengthened relationships. It can prevent stagnation and bring needed change in the lives of those who God has orchestrated to intersect our own path in life. As previously stated, conflict can't be completely avoided, but it can be managed and resolved. It can help us grow our skills at maintaining relationships. If a problem is not confronted, the conflict can escalate.

On another level, it's important to remember that many of our conflicts with others stem from a conflict we're having within ourselves. As I close this chapter, let's take a moment to explore these internal struggles. Whether you're a Christian or not, let's assume you have been exposed to God's word one way or another. Yet, despite your exposure to God's truth, you sometimes find yourself in situations that you know are wrong. By the time you realize you wanted to get out of the situation, it's way too late. It's like a ship that keeps veering off course when you're not looking—but the ship is you. You might do things that don't make sense to you, that upset you, and that make you feel horrified as you're doing them. You might feel like you're watching your life from outside, even as you're living it. Like you have this dark, secret identity and cannot be trusted. You might experience joy, love, and intimacy and then immediately feel sorrow at knowing that it could be taken away from you at any moment. You experience feelings of anxiety daily because you believe that moment when loss will happen is inevitable. You fear others will find out the truth eventually, so you live your life in a constant state of denial. This causes all your interactions with others to happen while you are in defense mode, and it seems like work to display your public persona.

When you're in constant pursuit of figuring out who you really are or even what motivates you, life becomes a vicious cycle of internal conflict. It takes a lot of energy just to start trying to reimagine something good and different for yourself. Maybe your cycle of self-torture has become so abbreviated that you cannot distinguish the difference between your true self and the destructive acts anymore. You might have a faint awareness that the acts are not what you want—that they hurt you, make you feel worthless and perhaps even disgusting. At times, you cannot believe you are the one capable of enacting them—but yet, there you are, once again. Doing the same things, acting like the person you told yourself you'd decided not to be. Life appears to be a thick and heavy fog of self-hate. That's when hopelessness emerges. Is there no end in sight?

The *why* behind this loop of behavior is rooted in the denial of the internal conflict that we choose not to confront. A denial of what we are ashamed to admit or are afraid to release (for a variety of reasons) when God's Spirit brings us to the point of conviction after we've heard the Word of Truth. These internal conflicts, like relational conflicts, are hard to resolve. They can betray us morally as well as spiritually, if we allow them. Conflict in any of life's situations can cause us to doubt God's goodness, His will for our lives, or His love for us. But, in fact, God uses conflict to refine our character, draw us closer to Him, and ultimately, to glorify Himself. God's biblical principles for confronting and resolving conflict can be applied to any type of conflict.

Conflicts often escalate because people don't follow God's biblical methods for resolving confrontation. We often dismiss God's methods because they don't quite make sense to us at first. God has made it clear that He does not think quite the same way as humans do, as we've seen in the previous chapter.

Perhaps looking at some examples of biblical personalities will be helpful here, to reveal what He expects from us. Hebrews 11 is often called the "Hall of Heroes." I refer to them as the "Heroes of Conflict and Confrontation." But the true hero in that chapter of Hebrews is God, who gives faith to His own. Even the smallest of men and women have overcome tremendous conflict and have achieved great things by relying on His strength. Their stories show why faith in God's Word (and trusting His reasoning) is so important. God's people are beset with weakness, poverty, and difficulty. Faith allows us to grasp the concept that God promises things that may be as yet unfulfilled in our experience. We hope for power in the midst of weakness, for peace in the midst of conflict, and for joy in the presence of sorrow. God requires His people to have faith to persevere in a difficult world.

In book of Hebrews the writer states, "By faith Abel offered to God a more excellent sacrifice than Cain, through which he obtained witness that he was righteous, God testifying of his gifts; and through it he being dead still speaks" (Hebrews 11:4 NKJV). But recall that God allowed Abel, the first human in the Bible to be referred to as "righteous," to be murdered. Was that reasonable?

Additionally, the writer says, "By faith Noah, being divinely warned of things not yet seen, moved with godly fear, prepared an ark for the saving of his household, by which he condemned the world and became heir of the righteousness which is according to faith" (Hebrews 11:7 NKJV). Look at what happened to Noah. God told him to build an ark, the biggest sailing vessel of all time. During his life, Noah was a "preacher of righteousness" (II Peter 2:5 NKJV), yet no one outside of his family listened to him. Was that reasonable?

Next, we are reintroduced to the father of the faithful. "By faith Abraham obeyed when he was called to go out to the place which he would receive as an inheritance. And he went out, not knowing where he was going" (Hebrews 11:8 NKJV). In Abraham's case, here we have a wealthy man living perhaps the most modern life possible at the time. And what did God tell him to do? God told him to leave most of his family and wander in the wilderness and live in tents (Genesis 12:1). Was that reasonable? God also told Abraham that he would have a child, but did not provide Isaac until Abraham was about a hundred years old. Was that reasonable?

The Bible tells us that, "By faith Joseph, when he was dying, made mention of the departure of the children of Israel, and gave instructions concerning his bones" (Hebrews 11:22 NKJV). What about Joseph? Here is a boy who, after God revealed a message to him in a dream, was hated by his brothers (Genesis 37 and 39). Here is an apparent teenager who, while doing what his father told him to do, was captured and thrown in a pit by his brothers and then sold into slavery. He then excelled as an outstanding servant-slave-leader. He resisted the advances of the adulterous spouse of Potiphar and his reward? Jail! Was that reasonable?

Lastly, "By faith Moses, when he became of age, refused to be called the son of Pharaoh's daughter, choosing rather to suffer affliction with the people of God than to enjoy the passing pleasures of sin" (Hebrews 11:24-25 NKJV). Because the Hebrews refused to support Moses (Acts 7:25), he apparently concluded that God was not going to need him. Forty years later, God drafted Moses against his will (Exodus 4:10-17). God repeatedly made Moses do things and be responsible for things that Moses did not want to do nor be responsible for. And because Moses got more upset one time than God thought he should have when the Israelites rebelled, God would not even let him enter the promised land (Deuteronomy 1:37) that he was seeking for forty additional years. Was that reasonable?

I began this chapter with the question, "Where is God in my darkest situations, when I need Him the most and can't sense His presence nor His will?" I trust that you now understand the reality of God's desire and power to bring hope out of the ashes of human conflicts and rebellions. Both His confrontation and His sacrificial love are meant to bring us back to Him, and He uses both in all of us. I often think of the metaphor used in Holy Scriptures of a callused, stubborn heart, and I imagine hearts frozen solid, cold toward God. It occurred to me that the judgment of God breaks up the ice frozen over our hearts, and the love of God melts the remaining clots of resistance and stubbornness that impede the flow of the Spirit in our lives.

Throughout life, you are going to go through many situations you may deem as unreasonable. Let me ask you to pray that God will confront you. Don't be afraid of His confrontation. His plan for you may materialize as conflicts about things that need to be judged in your life, things you're holding on to and covering up. Ask God to expose them so healing and restoration can take place. Also ask God to confirm your identity in Him. I hope we learn more and more how much God loves us, even during life's most undesirable situations. For the Christian, conflict is not something to avoid or ignore—it is an opportunity for the triumph of grace.

CHAPTER 3

DECISIONS, DECISIONS

When someone makes a decision,
he is really diving into a strong current that will carry him to places
he had never dreamed of when he first made the decision.
–Paulo Coelho, *The Alchemist*

I HAVE OFTEN WONDERED EXACTLY what the expression "decisions, decisions" means. There is no one exact definition for this phrase. When I have heard it in the past, it's been used as a "sentence" by itself, not as part of another sentence. "Decisions, decisions. Can't anyone do anything without my help?" Or, "Decisions, decisions. Why is choosing so hard?" More often than not, it is used when someone is complaining about having to make decisions. Sometimes it just means: "I have to make this decision before I take any action." It is not really a complaint. It is just a way of talking to oneself while trying to figure out what decision would be best.

We all want to make the right decisions. But we must understand how important it is for us to embrace the influence of the will of God, because the decisions we make in life will ultimately make us or break us. You may ask, "How can we know the will of God?" The phrase "the will of God" is used so loosely, that the consequence of that looseness impinges on our peace of mind. This is extremely serious. When we find ourselves suffering due to an ill-advised decision, we must train ourselves to trust, believe, and allow God to intervene. When we do, "we will discover that no evil circumstances can ever befall us that we cannot find in them a path which is God's way for us."[1]

In the summer of 1991, I too found myself mired in the valley of too many sticky decisions. I was walking along the cobblestone streets of downtown Savannah, Georgia, when an older gentleman who knew me from my radio broadcast called out to me: "Reverend Williams, you look like the weight of the world is on your shoulders," he observed with real concern in his voice. "Yes," I replied, "but I'm okay!" Little did he know I had spent the last two weeks struggling with a decision that would alter the trajectory of my future as I knew it at the time. I was surrounded by family discord and division, strained ministerial ties, strained relationships with friends and colleagues, and the gradual demise of all the current goals and aspirations I had planned for my life as a pastor.

The denomination in which I had grown up as a child—where I acknowledged my call to ministry and received the foundational development as a minister—was no longer a part of my life. Most of my ministry associates, friends, and family were calling and still reeling from my decision to pursue a new path for the future of my vocation. After twelve years of loyal and unwavering service, I had decided to follow through with what I discerned was God's plan for my life.

But I was no longer the carefree risk-taker with the backing of a solid denomination behind me. I no longer had the "family name" to depend upon. When I returned home, I looked in the bathroom mirror, and a thirty-two-year-old man stared back. How was I going to start over? As the question plagued my mind, fear began to grip my heart. Which course should I take? How would I know if I made the "right" decision? I shouldn't have been asking such questions. After all, I had heard from God—clearly. Right?

Standing on the brink of my life-changing decision, I wrestled with the pros and cons of my subsequent actions. How would I sift through the relevant factors, and separate them from the irrelevant? What role would my ministry play in God's plan now? Was I prepared to tackle the consequences of my decision and enter into this unknown dimension on my own?

I remember that time as if it were yesterday. It has been twenty-seven years. Looking back, I can now see God's reasoning. I thank God for His voice in my life. I would not be where I am today had I not listened to and obeyed God's voice. At the time of my decision, I wasn't struggling by any means. In fact, it was the very opposite. I was thriving as a young ambitious minister. By the account of everyone who knew me, I was in the ideal place to position myself for forward career movement and denominational promotion. But there was one problem. God was saying, "It's time to leave." Decisions of this magnitude are not easy, and unfortunately, the majority of people regard outside indicators as their internal rudders. Most allow impressions, emotions, or other pressure-packed forces to influence them. God knows I struggled with every one of them for a while. Then, one day, I decided to unequivocally trust God. I had to constantly remind myself that God has a long, successful track record of beautifying the bizarre, providing peace in the midst of pain, making something terrific from tragedy, and giving hope in the horrific.

It's hard to make good decisions if you don't know where you're going or haven't thought about what kind of person you want to become. For many people, the only criterion for deciding an issue is "What's easiest?" or "What do I feel like at the moment?" We all make many decisions every day—unconsciously or consciously. Sometimes we made a decision automatically, with little effort or thought. At other times, we agonize for hours. In our effort to do what is best, we tend to overlook any biases we

> If we really love God, we will increasingly love what He loves.

have or errors in our own judgment. Overconfidence, procrastination, immediate gratification, and limiting the search for viable answers are among the culprits that usually misguide our choices. Many individuals place great emphasis on the advice of others who validate their preferred choice. This only reinforces what could be a bad decision. So how do you make a solid, reliable decision without these kinds of negative influences? What is the missing component that would provide a sound basis for your decisions? The answer is found in the pages of Scripture. It is called wisdom, or the mind of God.

God supplies us with divine direction so we can make proper decisions through His wisdom. A secular view of wisdom might be defined today as: knowledge, the ability to discern inner qualities and relationships, insight, and judgment. However, biblical wisdom was described by the Hebrew word *chakmah*. This was more than just common sense. It was characterized by skill and craftsmanship, cleverness and cunning, and prudence in everyday matters. Wisdom graced the lives of many biblical figures, including Daniel, Ezra, and Joshua. It brought them great success. We would do well to follow their example of trust in God's divine direction over our decision-making.

I must admit that most of the decisions we must make on a daily basis aren't explicitly addressed in the Bible. The Bible doesn't give specific guidance on huge, life-shaping decisions. Should I enroll in the military, or go to college? How long should I remain single? Should I marry this person? Should we adopt a child? Should I pursue a different vocation? Should I pursue chemo, or try an alternative cancer treatment? Should I separate from my spouse while we work on these very painful issues?

These kinds of decisions tend to have multiple acceptable courses of action that fall within the scope of God's revealed moral will. Yet He also cares deeply about the details and courses of our daily lives. So what guidance does He give to help us navigate ambiguous decisions? He says, "Do not be conformed to this world, but be transformed by the renewal of your mind, that by testing you may discern what is the will of God, what is good and acceptable and perfect" (Romans 12:2 ESV).

What exactly does this mean, really? It means that God has a strategic plan. He knows we may have difficulty in discerning His will. The motives and affections of our hearts, or our "renewed minds," are more clearly revealed in cases of unguided decision-making. If God made the details of our situation more explicit, we would tend to focus more on what we do rather than what or who we love. Like the Pharisees, we would tend to whitewash our tombs to give the appearance of obedience or to impress others rather than to deal with the dead bones of our self-righteous pride.

But in decisions that require divine discernment, the wheat is distinguished from the tares. We make such decisions based on what and who we really love. If deep down we love the world, this will become apparent in the pattern of decisions that we make. We will conform to this world. But if we really love God, we will increasingly love what He loves. We will be transformed by renewed minds. And our love for Him and His kingdom will be revealed in the pattern of small and large decisions that we make.

Please note that I said "the pattern of decisions" because all of us sin and make occasional mistakes. But conformity to the world or to God is most clearly seen in the pattern of decisions we make over time. That's why God makes us wrestle. He wants us to mature and have our "powers of discernment trained by constantly practicing to distinguish good from evil" (Hebrews 5:14 ESV). But still, how can we determine the best choices to make, especially regarding big decisions and the ones that seemingly have no clear answer?

It's interesting to consider the decisions Abram (later called Abraham) and Lot made in a conflict situation, and the outcomes of those decisions. The story is told in the book of Genesis:

> "Lot, who was traveling with Abram, had also become very wealthy with flocks of sheep and goats, herds of cattle, and many tents. But the land could not support both Abram and Lot with all their flocks and herds living so close together. So disputes broke out between the herdsmen of Abram and Lot. (At that time Canaanites and Perizzites were also living in the land.)
>
> Finally Abram said to Lot, 'Let's not allow this conflict to come between us or our herdsmen. After all, we are close relatives! The whole countryside is open to you.

Take your choice of any section of the land you want, and we will separate. If you want the land to the left, then I'll take the land on the right. If you prefer the land on the right, then I'll go to the left.'

Lot took a long look at the fertile plains of the Jordan Valley in the direction of Zoar. The whole area was well watered everywhere, like the garden of the Lord or the beautiful land of Egypt. (This was before the Lord destroyed Sodom and Gomorrah.)

Lot chose for himself the whole Jordan Valley to the east of them. He went there with his flocks and servants and parted company with his uncle Abram. So Abram settled in the land of Canaan, and Lot moved his tents to a place near Sodom and settled among the cities of the plain. But the people of this area were extremely wicked and constantly sinned against the Lord.

After Lot had gone, the Lord said to Abram, 'Look as far as you can see in every direction—north and south, east and west. I am giving all this land, as far as you can see, to you and your descendants as a permanent possession.'"

(Genesis 13:5-15 NLT)

There's more to this story, of course. But it is interesting to note that God blessed Abram's generous decision for peace. Lot, on the other hand, did not see the spiritual danger he was putting his family in by choosing the fertile, but corrupt, area of Sodom.

Many decisions in life are like this. At the time, they don't seem significant. But those choices set in motion a series of events that shape your life and the lives of your children and grandchildren after you. The story of Lot teaches a crucial lesson about life's choices.

Since choices often result in eternally significant consequences, we must make every decision, no matter how small it seems, in line with God's principles. This brings us to the reason why it is so difficult to make God-designed decisions: it is because of the failure of competence on our part in acknowledging divine guidance. It has its deepest root in a failure to understand, accept, and grow into an authentic and trustworthy relationship with God. It is within such a relationship that our Lord surely intends us to have, and readily to recognize, His voice speaking in our hearts as occasion demands. Yet, we must acknowledge that there is a great paradox that exists

> God does not abandon those who make bad decisions.

concerning guidance. God speaks, and we are to obey His voice—and yet there is difficulty in discerning God's voice. Why?

I have been in ministry now for almost forty years, and I have come to the conclusion that there are three major causes of our inability to hear or to discern the voice of God:

1. Perhaps God is unable to reveal His will. In such a case, the problem would lie with Him.
2. Perhaps there is sinfulness or insincerity on our part. Then, obviously, we would be the cause of our own failure.
3. Perhaps our understanding of the nature of God's will is biblically deficient. If that were true, then the problem would be ignorance.

We can rule out cause number one, because God is never the problem. Causes number two and three are the culprits of our deafness toward the voice of God. Satan uses the tools of sinfulness, insincerity, and ignorance to block the voice of God in our decision-making processes. Satan wants to destroy you! He wants to rob you of your blessings and ultimately interfere with your destiny. So make that choice not to let the enemy win! Stand on God's Word and seek God's will! Make the right decisions!

God doesn't just want you to make the right decisions, however, He wants to guide you as you make it so you learn along the way.

In other words, God knows what is best for you, and He wants to reveal it to you and show you what you ought to do. God has a better plan in mind for all of us than what we can create from our finite perspective. For instance, the Holy Spirit told Philip to go to a desert road in the middle of nowhere—even while a great revival was occurring in Samaria (Acts 8:26), but it must not have been clear to him why God wanted him to do that. Also, when Paul made a good and reasonable decision to preach the gospel in Asia, the Holy Spirit blocked it from happening (Acts 16:6). Paul was the greatest leader in the early church, but God allowed him to spend significant time locked in prison. As it turns out, Paul ended up leading most of his prison guards to Christ, and this helped spread Christianity to the Roman world (Phil. 1:13).

We must come to a place where we realize that every God-informed decision is infused with a God-purpose beyond what we could ever know or understand. We must also embrace the fact that a good idea does not always stem from God—no matter how much time you spent meditating on it, praying on it, or even fasting to come up with that idea. Sometimes, after a long period of thoughtful, reasonable, and prayerful reflection, we will still make a decision that God will want to override. In these cases, we can trust that God will "close a door," so to speak. Sometimes, if we are being stubborn with pushing our agenda, God will allow us to choose our own path. But if we are really searching for His will, we can be confident that He will stop opportunities from happening in order get our attention.

It seems people are constantly running up against the consequences of bad decisions. Try as we might, some things just do not work out. Our decisions also frequently yield unintended results. Resolving problems after the fact can be difficult enough, but what happens when our bad decisions involve God's will? Specifically, what happens when we are overtly disobedient to Him? Here is the good news about bad decisions: God does not abandon those who make bad decisions. Even overtly sinful decisions can be overcome, and those mistakes can lead us to a new experience of God's grace.

The truth is, you and I are very capable of making a bad decision.

Bad decisions have consequences. More often than not, bad decisions lead us into the seasons of our lives where we, like others before us, find ourselves attempting to find some level of comfort by quoting the phrase "everything happens for a reason." I catch myself saying this at times when, as a counselor, I am attempting to bring a sense of calm to a chaotic situation. Although, in the proper context, there is some truth in that phrase. As it relates to an individual facing the consequences of a poor decision, there is the danger of missing the fact that the real reason is the direct result of a poor decision. In reality, this has very little to do with God's will. Even though God didn't cause it to happen, He did, and still does, have the ability to change the end result. As such, it might be better for us to understand that God has the ability to bring reason to everything that happens.

King Solomon said, "Let the wise listen and add to their learning, and let the discerning get guidance" (Proverbs 1:5 NIV). Sometimes failure can be the best teacher. As God brings reason to even our poor decisions, allow His wisdom to take root in your mind and begin to learn from your mistakes. Allow the lesson of missing the mark to be a guide in the future. Start walking with God even when you recognize that you are wrong. Trust Him to straighten what you made crooked as you fully surrender to Him. But surrender *fully*, by all means. (There is no such thing as partial surrender.) Take responsibility for your own actions and invite God into your situations daily—even moment by moment.

Most Christians are familiar with the life story David, the son of Jesse the Bethlehemite. David's story of how God developed his faith, that he could serve his ultimate purpose, is filled with peaks and valleys. One day King David made a horrible decision, by choosing to commit adultery with Bathsheba and murdering her husband. Because of that decision, the child who was conceived died. David was rebuked by Nathan the prophet. There were dire consequences for the decision David made. In response, he humbly admitted his guilt, repented, and was restored. After this event, God declared David to be "a man after His own heart." God brought redemption to a destructive decision. It was Solomon, the son who was later born to David and Bathsheba and who succeeded David as king, who built the temple and achieved an unsurpassed measure of success. Even though David paid a great price for his poor decision, the redemptive work of God is evident. He ultimately brought about a blessed result that David's actions did not warrant—that's grace.

The worst thing in the world you—or anyone else—can do after making a bad decision that came from either not pursuing or from ignoring God's counsel is to let that pattern continue. Turn it around immediately and vehemently, with true repentance and complete surrender to God. This is the beginning of all lasting change. Remember, it was foolish rebellion that got King David in trouble. Foolish neglect or rebellion, if repeated, will do nothing but wreak further havoc, pain, hardship, and misery on you and those around you.

The wonderful thing to remember as we set about making decisions is that Jesus is our Good Shepherd. He laid down his life for us so that all of our sins (including every sinful or defective decision) are covered. He will never leave or forsake us. He has a staff long enough to pull us out of every hole and a rod to guide us back when we stray. And someday, we will see that it really was Him leading us through the confusing terrain of difficult decisions.

CHAPTER 4

FIGHT OR FLIGHT

*Fear was the hand of the devil holding a scalding hot branding iron
and touching your brain and your stomach
and yelling at you to run with leaden feet.*
— Dan Groat, *Monarchs and Mendicants*

AS WAS DISCUSSED IN CHAPTER 2, confrontation is always difficult, and often necessary. It is something that many of us do badly—or avoid at all costs. We tend to default toward one of two paths: either we run from confrontation, or we find ourselves continually confronting everything. This is our fight or flight response. It doesn't take too long to realize that both of these methods, however, are more often than not ineffective at solving problems.

Confrontation can come in the form of loss of employment, separation or divorce, chronic disease, increasing medical expenses, a death in the family, or an argument or fight with a friend or family member. Circumstances such as these—and too many others to name here—create pressures that cause stress in the lives of adults, teenagers, and children. Stress is unavoidable in today's hectic world. In fact, if you're like most people I know, you could be an excellent candidate for a diagnosis of stress overload.

Relationships, Life Experiences, and the Urge of "Fight or Flight"

Relationships—and life as a whole—are hard. Because of that, Satan uses them as major points of attack. Maintaining a healthy lifestyle and a pleasant coexistence with other human beings, even those you care deeply about, is challenging. Life and relationships change over time and are subject to the inevitable enemy of peace: problems. Problems in any area of life make us mindful of all our feelings, including our painful feelings. Satan first attacks our emotions in order to establish the foundation for his subsequent strategies. Rather than avoiding them or trying to forget about them by giving in to ungodly urges, you must make a conscious decision to take responsibility for your feelings. You may be causing your own anxiety, depression, anger, guilt, and shame with your own thoughts and actions. You must take responsibility for learning how to combat and heal painful feelings—the fear, danger, loneliness, heartbreak, helplessness, and grief. This begins the process of opening us up to receive the spiritual gifts that can enliven and sustain us.

Courage, compassion, love, joy, peace, patience, kindness, goodness, faithfulness, gentleness, self-control—these are the regenerated feelings that stem from our true spiritual essence when we are connected with the Spirit of God. These feelings are what the Spirit is, what God is. These feelings are gifts of the Spirit that we experience when we allow them to be released in moments of stress or distress. We can open our hearts to receiving these gifts, and make ourselves open to learning about loving and responding not only to our own feelings, but also others'.

While this is the regenerated state of the redeemed soul when connected with the Spirit of God, it is not our natural state of the mind. We experience our primitive fallen nature first, and respond to life with base instincts for survival in a fallen world. It is what we use to control people and the outcome of things, often through some form of "fight or flight" response. The "fight or flight" response is known as an acute stress response. It refers to a physiological reaction that occurs in the presence of something that is terrifying, either mentally or physically. It is also the response of the body to a perceived threat. Both of these tendencies are very natural for our flesh, but neither of these ways are pleasing to the Lord. This is because they do not benefit our spiritual growth. In fact, they hinder it.

Some common emotional manifestations of fight or flight are: anger, blame, withdrawal, resistance, rebellion, and competitiveness. The Apostle Paul addresses the shift we need to make to our mindset in order to live in the realm of God in his writings to the church in Rome (Romans 12:2). Paul speaks of transformation as consisting of a renewal of the mind, which indicates that there must be a higher understanding, or thinking power, to guide moral activity. And the Christian "mind renewal" process imparts not only the will and power to do God's will, but also the intelligence to discern how to adapt. The renewing of your mind is not accomplished by merely professing an outward disconformity to a fallen and ungodly world, but by an inward spiritual transformation that makes your whole life new—new in its motives and ends.

With all the stresses and pressures of life, we must guard our thought life while we are engaging in the mind-renewal process. Although we might submit our life to God, it does not mean we will be completely exempt from feeling "fight or fight" responses sometimes. Challenges in life are normal and to be expected. But we all have to contend with one of the most critical challenges in this world: choosing what path we walk on in this life and how we walk that path. We are either on a freeing spiritual journey, humbling ourselves to the will and the way of God's sovereign leadership, or enslaved to the earthly journey, where control over our actions is determined by our fallen, flawed nature and a fallen world. Our intent in learning about life or trying to have control over getting what we want in life while avoiding pain governs which journey we are on *in any given moment.*

When our intent is trying to control our own destiny, our untransformed mind is in charge. When our intent is to learn God's will concerning our destiny, our regenerated righteous heart is in charge. When we choose consciously to learn about God's will, our heart opens to the mind and the gifts of the Spirit of God. This may sound easy, yet it is a constant challenge because we have to choose the intent to learn moment by moment.

Jesus put it this way: "Come unto me, all ye that labour and are heavy laden, and I will give you rest. Take my yoke upon you, and learn of me; for I am meek and lowly in heart: and ye shall find rest unto your souls. For my yoke is easy, and my burden is light" (Matthew 11:28-30 KJV). The yoke of Jesus is all about the heart and mind. When we shape ourselves in the image of Jesus, we become meek and gentle in all our dealings. Jesus equips us to deal with egos that would otherwise drive us to all kinds of excesses. He helps us bring every thought and every action under the control. He helps us love spiritual things more than we love the world. When we first put on the yoke of Jesus, it is strangely uncomfortable and disturbing. But as time passes, it begins to feel natural until it eventually seems to be a part of us—one we could not function without.

The yoke has another implication: it's a metaphor for experience linked with the new information we are exposed to during the mind-transformation process we undergo when we begin to seek God's word. If we never had new experiences to link with the new information of God's Holy Scriptures, human nature would take advantage of the second-biggest influence on learning: our emotional responses to any given situation. Experiences in life, good or bad, are a vital part of the process of learning to walk a spiritual path. Remember, learning is a social behavior; God plans and orchestrates life lessons through challenging experiences. It's up to us to make connections to the scriptures we've read and studied for the renewing of our minds. That is how we can learn to forego "fight or flight" responses and instead turn to a God-facilitated learning process. Doing so will help us thrive, not merely survive. "Fight or flight" is about survival, not winning! It is about being a victim, not a victor! God's desire for us is that we live an abundant life, not settle for a mundane existence.

Instincts and the Urge of "Fight or Flight"

"Fight or flight" thrives on our natural instincts. If you put all the world's trouble into a big pot and boil it down, it reduces to a conflict between those who are governed by their own natural instincts and those who are governed by the Holy Spirit of God. Belief in God and our dependence on His Holy Spirit are a product of our evolved spiritual intelligence. Holy Scripture gives us the means to turn to God, who is all-powerful, all-loving, and fair, during times of adversities, losses, and hardships. These things easily overwhelm nonbelievers in the struggle to survive in this world.

Among all the emotions we are capable of expressing, fear is the common denominator. Fear can be an extremely effective motivator. Many of us have seen, heard, or experienced something so fearsome that our "fight or flight" response kicked in. The terror moved us to take immediate steps to defend ourselves physically or to seek protection by running from the danger.

Take a look into the Bible with me to see how a key disciple of Jesus Christ responded in difficult times—Apostle Peter. "Then Simon Peter, having a sword, drew it and struck the high priest's servant, and cut off his right ear" (John 18:10 ESV). Peter exhibited fight mode when he chopped off the ear of the high priest's servant. I'm sure God wants us to rely on His word to handle life's challenging situation. Now you may not opt to cut off someone's ear, but I'm sure at some point in time you would have loved to slap someone! Or maybe use some stabbing words to get back at them? Am I alone in this, or can you relate? Okay, okay, let me advise you to take a step back from that moment and harken to the word of the Lord: "'In your anger do not sin': Do not let the sun go down while you are still angry, and do not give the devil a foothold." (Ephesians 4:26-27 NIV).

On another occasion, Peter displayed flight mode when he denied knowing the Lord three times for fear he would be taken into custody just like Jesus: "But Peter said, 'Man, I do not know what you are saying!' Immediately, while he was still speaking, the rooster crowed.

And the Lord turned and looked at Peter. Then Peter remembered the word of the Lord, how He had said to him, 'Before the rooster crows, you will deny Me three times.' So, Peter went out and wept bitterly" (Luke 22:60-62 NKJV). The man took off. He bailed. He ran away. Sometimes it's just easier to not deal with

> Satan first attacks our emotions in order to establish the foundation for his subsequent strategies.

things than to face them, isn't it? Fear will have that effect on you from time to time. But God does not want us to handle our life situations by relying on fight or flight mode.

Is it possible for Christians to have another response to turmoil in addition to these normal "human-wired" reactions? David, in Psalm 31 (NIV), wrote that he was in distress and anguish, experiencing sorrow and loneliness, but he went on to say, "I trust in you, Lord . . . My times are in your hands . . . the Lord showed me the wonders of His love when I was in a city under siege." Although the "fight or flight" response is helpful in cases of physical threat (such as needing to run away from a rabid dog or an angry panther), it is however inappropriate and maladaptive when it occurs during life situations He orchestrates for our development. No human power alone can stop the devil's schemes, but God can and has already "disarmed the rulers and authorities and put them to open shame, by triumphing over them in him" (Colossians 2:15 ESV). The paths we take when we are presented with various temptations will differ, but the principle is the same: seek to find refuge in God, through your relationship with Christ and His Word.

When faced with a difficult choice, we have all probably heard this advice: "Oh, just go with your instincts" or "Your instincts are never wrong." Does that sound familiar? Well, my relationship with God has corrected me concerning this ill-advised statement. It is flawed! Tom Stella, in his book *The God Instinct: Heeding Your Heart's Unrest*, said those who seek for answers to the innate longings of our nature are "moved in a conscious and intentional manner to hold this desire as a priority and to pursue its fulfillment."[1] But it is necessary that we look beyond this life and our world for the satisfaction of this inner urging.

There are times in our lives when our instincts, however pure they may seem, are dead wrong. For example, in 2008, I was nearing the end of a return trip to Boca Raton, Florida, from Washington, DC. I had been on the road for fourteen straight hours. As I passed the Fort Pierce exit on I-95, there was a tornado warning. The radio message alert said the tornado was just a short distance north of that very exit. It was dark and raining heavily. My instincts were telling me to pull over with all the other cars at the exit ramp. But the Holy Spirit came to me at that very moment and urged me to do something entirely different—advance forward!

At that moment, there was a conflict going on in me between my instincts and my spiritual guide and counselor. All my mental and emotional instincts were telling me to pull over, to align myself along the side of the road and wait out the storm with everyone else. I continued on, passed the exit, and the road ahead of me was clear of cars because they had all stopped. I could feel the wind speed increase. I continued to drive through the heavy rains and the strong winds for about two or three miles. Suddenly, the bad weather conditions began to subside. The rain began to lift, and the skies cleared. Once I arrived home, the news channels reported that the tornado hit I-95 at the very location my instincts had been telling me to stop. The cars that had stopped were unfortunately involved in the turmoil, and many of them became victims of the devastation the tornado left behind. If I had listen to those instincts, I would have placed myself and my vehicle in danger.

Then there are times our instincts tell us to flee when we shouldn't. We often feel this battle when something we're engaged in is too exhausting and overwhelming. We feel that we don't have enough energy or aren't fully equipped to fight. We think we're too tired, too old, too young, too sick, too weak. We believe the problem is bigger than our resources or personal abilities. It is then that we need the reasoning of God more than ever.

God offers truth and peace in every situation. YOU WERE

NEVER MEANT TO FIGHT ALONE! Paul makes our source of power and strength clear in Ephesians chapter 6. It is God, Himself, who holds the power to fight and win. Verse 10 commands us to "be strong in the Lord and in the strength of his might."

In the next several verses of Ephesians 6, we see that God has provided spiritual protective equipment for us to use in circumstances of perceived threat to our Christian experience. I'm sure some of us are familiar with this passage, and the ways in which God intends for His saints to be protected and to defend themselves:

> "Put on the whole armor of God, that you may be able to stand against the schemes of the devil. For we do not wrestle against flesh and blood, but against the rulers, against the authorities, against the cosmic powers over this present darkness, against the spiritual forces of evil in the heavenly places. Therefore take up the whole armor of God, that you may be able to withstand in the evil day, and having done all, to stand firm. Stand therefore, having fastened on the belt of truth, and having put on the breastplate of righteousness, and, as shoes for your feet, having put on the readiness given by the gospel of peace. In all circumstances take up the shield of faith, with which you can extinguish all the flaming darts of the evil one; and take the helmet of salvation, and the sword of the Spirit, which is the word of God, praying at all times in the Spirit, with all prayer and supplication. To that end, keep alert with all perseverance, making supplication for all the saints,…"
>
> (Ephesians 6:10-20 ESV)

So, after taking inventory of the equipment we need to engage in strategic spiritual warfare with the devil, I noticed something that could be detrimental to our spiritual health if overlooked. Of the six vital pieces of armor mentioned, there's only one actual weapon that we can use to defend ourselves. One: the sword of the Spirit. This one item just became that much more important. Why? If you don't learn how to use the sword of the Spirit, then how are you going to defend yourself from the wiles of the devil? The Apostle Paul's implication in this verse is that if you don't employ God's word in your life, you will spend your entire Christian experience on the defensive, running away from the attacks of the devil instead of standing to face him, as Paul commands us to do in the text.

In this spiritual warfare that rages over individual souls, what we want more than anything else is to conquer Satan and to escape the hands of evil men and women who carry out his work. It is when we are lost in the mists of darkness and cannot find our way that we most desperately need the influence of the Lord.

As a first-aid or prevent maintenance kit to our spiritual armor, I cannot stress too highly the protective power that comes into our lives through earnest, humble, consistent, yearning prayer. You need to find a time and place where you can be alone with our Heavenly Father and pour out your heart to Him, that you might add strength and power to your spiritual lives. Every honest and sincere prayer strengthens another piece of your armor.

CHAPTER 5

FULL DISCLOSURE

Come near to God and he will come near to you. Wash your hands, you sinners, and purify your hearts, you double-minded.
—James 4:8 (NIV)

"FULL DISCLOSURE" IS A PHRASE that gets tossed about quite a bit these days. It always seems to arouse strong opinions in people. There are those who believe that there are some things that are best left unsaid, and that revealing what they consider to be unnecessary detail is just asking for trouble. Then there are those who believe that withholding any information—especially about one's past—is a form of dishonesty. Accompanying this belief is the innate disturbing feeling that if or when that past is made known from any other source, the person's character is called into question, his or her reputation becomes tainted, and the damage to trust levels in relationships can be extreme—and sometimes irreparable.

I define full disclosure within relationships as a willingness to reveal, on an ongoing basis, our thoughts, feelings, concerns, desires, and needs—that is, whatever aspects of our ongoing experience are relevant to that current relationship. Disclosure has at least as much to do with what is happening with us every day as it has to do with what we've done in the past.

This requires each person in the relationship to have developed the capacity for self-reflection and self-awareness of their own moment-to-moment experience. This awareness doesn't require us to continually uncap our mental reservoir of thoughts and flush out every feeling we have, but it does have to do with a willingness to do so when what is going on within us is relevant to our relationship. To withhold such information could diminish the quality of the connection with the other person, including the level of trust, understanding, and intimacy.

Most individuals are generally not honest with themselves. It is because we're afraid that blunt honesty will land us in hot water. It is the opposite with God. Because of Jesus, we don't have to be afraid to be honest . . . because honesty has been turned into a pathway to a fulfilled life. But the question we have to wrestle with is: How honest am I with God? Most of us edit our conversations with Him. We sanitize our emotions because we don't want to offend or anger

> Your thoughts matter to God as much as your actions.

Him. But what if God wants us to be honest with Him? What if he values full disclosure over decorum? The answer is simple. James, the apostle, is quite forthcoming on this topic: "Come near to God and he will come near to you. Wash your hands, you sinners, and purify your hearts, you double-minded" (James 4:8 NIV). Until we are willing to be fully honest with God, we are not going to experience God fully. God desires to be intimately close with us, but the conditions are clear.

God knows our thoughts. Every single one of them, good and bad. Every proposal you consider, every scheme you contemplate, every image you imagine (good, bad, natural, or spiritual). It is all seen and heard by your Heavenly Father. So, you may ask, "What's the point in me sharing with God what He already knows?" It is important to remember that God judges your mental integrity just as meticulously as He judges your conversations and actions. If you don't believe it, let's take a look at a few scriptures that shed some light on this topic:

"Let the words of my mouth, and the meditation of my heart, be acceptable in thy sight, O Lord, my strength, and my redeemer."

(Psalms 19:14 KJV)

"The thoughts of the wicked are an abomination to the Lord: but the words of the pure are pleasant."

(Proverbs 15:26 KJV)

"O Jerusalem, wash thine heart from wickedness, that thou mayest be saved. How long shall thy vain thoughts lodge within thee?"

(Jeremiah 4:14 KJV)

"And thou, Solomon my son, know thou the God of thy father, and serve him with a perfect heart and with a willing mind: for the LORD searcheth all hearts, and understandeth all the imaginations of the thoughts: if thou seek him, he will be found of thee; but if thou forsake him, he will cast thee off forever."

(1 Chronicles 28:9 KJV)

Your thoughts matter to God as much as your actions. Learn to control them for His glory. As you go throughout your day, understand that God knows your thoughts. The question we must all ask ourselves is: "Is He happy with what He sees and hears in my head?"

The Apostle Paul writes in Hebrews, "And no creature is hidden from his sight, but all are naked and exposed to the eyes of him to whom we must give account" (Hebrews 4:13 ESV). Scriptures like this used to seriously frighten me. The idea that an all-powerful, all-knowing, and perfectly holy God knew everything I had ever done seemed at first too intrusive for me. He didn't even need my permission to invade my private thoughts. So, if I couldn't even muster up the courage to truly be myself to man, how could I handle being "naked and exposed" before my Heavenly Father?

Heart Posturing

The key to achieving full disclosure with God is posturing our heart to reveal that which He already knows to be true. It is about our integrity with God. Here is the good news: God's goodness far exceeds anything we've experienced in our lives on earth. We have only splashed around in the shallows of God's deep pool of love and mercy. In order to dive deeper into the fullness of life available to us, we must learn how to posture our hearts.

It is paramount that we endeavor to spread our lives out, uninhibited and transparent, before God because He will not address what is not true. He will not flirt with us in misconception, and He will not nurture any false projection of ourselves. He will not meet with that which doesn't truly exist. Brennan Manning writes in his book *Abba's Child: The Cry of the Heart for Intimate Belonging*,[1] "The false self is frustrated because he never hears God's voice. He cannot, since God sees no one there." Thomas Merton says of the false self, "This is the man I want myself to be but who cannot exist, because God does not know anything about him"[2]

Honesty is a virtue that is not automatic to us. Nor does it grow in a moment. Honesty is a trait that has to be developed over time. It grows by practice. Jesus noted these things in his comment recorded in Luke's gospel: "One who is faithful in a very little is also faithful in much, and one who is dishonest in a very little is also dishonest in much" (16:10 ESV). This comment implies a growth process. One can see that persistent honesty, or being faithful over and over again, is what produces the kind of effect God wants from us.

The life of Abraham is the prototypical tale about how faith develops. His life experience with God appears early in the Old Testament, and then in Genesis 22:1-12 focuses on how he confirms his faith. You will notice that this is not the first story about Abraham, however. It is preceded by many other stories, some of which indicate great faithfulness in following after God, and others that expose his failures.

The story in Genesis chapter 22 is very significant, because it comes well after some of Abraham's failures. He and Sarah now have the family God promised, in their son Isaac. Then in a apparent instance of God's unreasonable reasoning comes the command for Abraham to take his young son to Mount Moriah to make a sacrifice. At some point along the way, Abraham learns he is to sacrifice Isaac. Anyone who reads this story today is greatly alarmed by God's request, but it was not out of the realm of reality in Abraham's day. In the end, God prevented the sacrifice of the young man, then provided Abraham with a substitute sacrifice.

> Trust is an essential aspect of the God-man relationship.

There is great significance to this story, but for the purpose of understanding the importance of full disclosure in our relationship with God, let's look at the fact that Abraham was willing to obey God. We can conclude that, as his life progressed, he learned to be honest with God, heeding of God's admonitions. For this, God commended Abraham not only during his time with Him under the Old Covenant, but also in Hebrews 11, often called the "Hall of Faith" or the "Faith Hall of Fame" under the New Covenant. Abraham receives much more than a brief mention among the pantheon of heroes of faith. A good deal of emphasis (from Hebrews 11:8-19) is given to this biblical giant and father of the Jewish nation, hence God's acknowledgement of Abraham's full disclosure of his heart by virtue of his obedience.

Theology of Conscience and Accountability

Our Christian argument in favor of full disclosure is rooted in a theology of conscience that can be supported by the biblical principle of cooperation. God alone is the Lord of the conscience. Apostle Paul strongly advocated that, "the aim of our charge is love that issues from a pure heart, and a good conscience, and a sincere faith." Doubtless heart, conscience, and faith are closely related. In the New Testament, the discussion of a good heart is not missing, but the idea of a good conscience is known to stem from confidence and serenity. Paul is sure this is a good idea. He says, "I always take pains to have a clear conscience toward God and man." He references this idea often, for example: "I thank God whom I serve with a clear conscience," "holding faith and a good conscience," and "holding the mystery of the faith with a clear conscience." Another revealing statement is, "I am speaking the truth in Christ, I am not lying; my conscience bears me witness in the Holy Spirit" (See: I Tim. 1:5, Acts 24:16, II Tim. 1:3, I Tim. 1:19, Rom. 9:1).

The problem that Christians struggle with daily as they try to apply Gospel values to a broken and imperfect world is that, for many, the full disclosure issue and a good conscience may not fall within their realm of cooperation with God. The question then is whether or not cooperation is formal. Is it visible? This distinction is central to the principle of cooperation and the theology of conscience. Formal cooperation consists in the consent to a deed performed which may or may not involve actual participation in the material action of the deed; whereas visible (material) cooperation requires active participation in the deed performed. In essence, formal cooperation lacks not only action, it also lacks heart and conviction—it is empty and self-promoting. Visible cooperation values substance, purpose, and accountability.

Because formal cooperation is not based on moral conditions such as right or wrong, our relationship with God can be defined under material cooperation. Everything God has promised us within our covenant with Him is based on conditions. It is His way of testing our faithfulness and purity of heart. He requires all of us to submit to His conditions and, in return for our cooperation under these conditions, we have the promise of His influence, involvement, and ultimate blessings in every area of life.

Visible cooperation requires the moral responsibility of aligning our walk and our conscience with the perfect will of God and with all that entails, including respecting His process, fulfilling His requirements, and maintaining trust in Him. Trust is an essential aspect of the God-man relationship, which could be seriously undermined by withholding any part of yourself from God. As we submit to full disclosure and trust in God, we move in cooperation with His plan for our life while He provides the guidance we need in times of great need.

Beware! Visible cooperation without a moral God-conscience is empty and futile. It is flesh driven and lacks the possibility of a sustainable commitment. Robert Sokolowski said, "We must begin to speak of a theology that investigates appearances. The average individual will immediately suppose that we intend to examine 'merely' the way things appear, not the way they are. When one tries to describe and carry out the theology of disclosure, one is obliged to work against deeply ingrained prejudices that distort both our religious and our cultural understanding."[3]

It is my conviction that our accountability to God places a demand on us as Christians to commit to examine ourselves daily. We must align our relationship with Him according to His values and standards, because one day we will all be required to give an account of our lives. To me, one of the most interesting verses in the Gospels is a statement by Jesus in Luke 12:47-48. Jesus gives a parable about a wise servant and another who is evil. In the parable, the Lord says that His servants will one day give an account to Him. He concludes the parable with these words:

> "From everyone who has been given much, much will be demanded; and from the one who has been entrusted with much, much more will be asked."
> (Luke 12:48b NIV)

Those who have more knowledge of what Christ requires and the reasons for those requirements have a greater responsibility to act in an enlightened way. The parable emphasizes that privilege brings responsibility, and that responsibility entails accountability. Even in the fourth century BC, Plato touched upon the subject of anonymity and morality in his parable of the ring of Gyges. That mythical ring gave its owner the power of invisibility, and Plato speculated that even a habitually just man who possessed such a ring would quickly become a thief, knowing that he couldn't be caught. Morality in its purest form, Plato argues, comes from full disclosure; without risk of being held accountable for our actions, we would all behave unjustly.

Until we are honest and accountable to God about who we are and how we feel, we will never be able to understand who He is and how He feels. Throughout the Bible, we read about the reciprocating nature of God. There's something about us bringing our full selves to God that allows us to access, grasp, and experience all of God in return. We know this in our mind, but sometimes certain situations compel us to want to trust ourselves more than we trust God. In Romans 11:32-35, Paul reminds us of the depth and riches of God's wisdom and knowledge: "how unsearchable *are* His judgments and His ways past finding out!" He asks some rhetorical questions:

- "Who has known the mind of the Lord?" We can't, unless He shares it.
- "Who has become His counselor?" Nobody.
- "Who has first given to Him so that He owes you?" Nobody.

Paul continues to remind us that: "From Him, through Him, and to Him are all things." We can fully trust Him with our suppressed issues, weaknesses, and any challenges that confront us today. It will keep us from looking to our fallible selves—or elsewhere—for the answers that only God can supply.

CHAPTER 6

WHEN ONE DOOR CLOSES

*If God closes a door AND a window, consider the fact that
it might be time to build a whole new house.*
— Mandy Hale, *The Single Woman*

CAN YOU THINK OF A time in your life when God slammed a
door shut right in your face? It can be hard to remain steadfast and
hopeful when it feels like every time you get close to something that
resembles a breakthrough for your life, God allows it to be snatched
it away. Put another way, every time you take a step in the right
direction, life forces you take two steps backward. Constant repeating
cycles of being pushed back to square one is no fun. It can be very
stressful at times. It can drain you of your faith in God's plan. But
I want to begin this chapter by saying up front that the end goal of
God's intentions in the matter is always for our good.

God wants to tell a story through your life. It unfolds as doors
open and close. There is even a saga beginning in your life right
now—and you may or may not be aware of it. It is the spiritual
order of God's progressive plan for His creation. One of my favorite
authors, Max Lucado, says that: "Your story indwells God's . . .
above and around us God directs a grand saga, written by His hand,
orchestrated by His will, unveiled according to His calendar. And
you are a part of it." [1]

In 2013, I had two major doors shut in my face. One door was a new ministry position that would have been perceived as a career advancement, and the other was a possible connection with a person of affluence, which would also have added name recognition to my growing network of ministerial associates. These possibilities seemed to be sure things at first, and the doors appeared to be wide open. Walking through those doors would have changed the trajectory of my life.

I was so close to the opportunities, I could taste them. I saw the openings clearly. Like many Christians love to say, I prayed about them, sought God's counsel concerning them, fine-tuned my spiritual sensitivities for clarity concerning them. I was convinced that God had indeed swung both doors open and cleared my path through them. Or so I thought! Imagine how it felt to have them both slam shut and closed tight. No amount of desire on my part could reopen them.

Honestly, it shook the foundation of my Bible-thumping, faith-slinging, God-fearing world. It hurt. It knocked me over like a boulder pried away from its secure place on the side of a mountaintop. For weeks, the resounding thud resonated in my heart's chambers. The disappointment and the pain were very real. It happens to us all, and there is no getting around it.

When doors close in our life, it hurts us both spiritually and emotionally. There is a reason for our dislike of closed doors! They represent the one thing we all would like to avoid: rejection. Perhaps the hardest and the harshest word we ever heard growing up was in fact the shortest: "No." Such a small, two-letter word, but it is packed with an enormous amount of power. It always elicits an emotional response, and the outcome of its intended purpose is always hurtful to some degree. "No" has the dual ability to both prevent and protect, of course. The second meaning is rarely our immediate interpretation of why it's being used when someone confronts us with that word.

Do you know what it's like to ask God for something and to keep receiving a "no" in return? I certainly do. When we hear the word "no," something happens internally that shakes us to the core. We feel disappointment. It comes in waves. This ebb and flow of emotions allows us to touch the brink of insanity or despair, but not quite to cross over the delicate edge. [2] I have discovered that when I feel disappointed by God, it is because at that moment there's something I'm longing for more than Him.

I grew up in the small town of St. Mary's, in southeastern Georgia. I was able to experience the few and simple pleasures that made life meaningful. So when, as a child, I would ask for the privilege of doing something I thought would be fun and pleasurable or when I sought permission to have something I viewed as a must-have, "no" was not a welcomed response. It wasn't until I was a young adult, responsible for my own life and its outcomes, that God taught me the preventative *and* protective interpretations of this answer. Our human *will* almost singularly sees the preventative side of "no" as merely a barrier restricting us, when in fact, God's "no" is always the gateway to another door that He designed for you—He is directing you down a better path for the best outcome.

Parents often say: "No, don't touch that electrical outlet," "No, don't touch that hot stove," or "No, do not play in the middle of the street." Our youthful ignorance and curiosity blind us to the protective impulse behind those words. In our moment of playful desire, we only feel prevented from doing something we very much want to do.

We often see God's closed doors the same way. At times, we

> The door that God opens will be accompanied by confirmation.

even try to turn God's words around and use them against Him by quoting scriptures out of context. "But God! You said You would give me the desires of my heart!" "You said, 'Ask anything in Jesus's name'—give it to me!'" When God says no to us, we often react like a child throwing a temper tantrum. We see it as another instance of Him preventing us from enjoying life or perhaps of standing in the way of fulfilling our dreams.

I'm of the opinion that the reason closed doors hurt so much is because we have a plan for our lives and we are always in pursuit of that "ideal life" that we ourselves have designed. We have arrogantly approved and confirmed what we want, ahead of God's input. I'll share an important life principle to embrace and learn, and the sooner you do, the sooner you will be at peace with all of God's "no's." Are you ready? Here it goes: When our loving, Heavenly Father sees us rushing into something that is outside of His will or planning something that will ultimately not be in our best interest, He WILL slam that door closed.

All too often, we become obsessed with what we want or what could have been. We attempt to ram our way through a closed door or squeeze ourselves into a place we don't belong. This could be maintaining a relationship with a person who was never meant for us, or pursuing a dream that is not God's destiny for us. The outcome, however, is always the same: whether it takes a long or short period of time, we learn that there was a reason that door was closed.

Yes, when the door first closes, it may lead to hurt, discontentment, heartbreak, and what feel like missed opportunities. It may even cause us to second-guess ourselves and question God in the process. And that is where the misery concerning our relationship and spiritual standing with God begins. We struggle with questions like: Am I that out of touch with God's will? Did I misunderstand His voice that much? Did I do something wrong? Did I move out of alignment with God so much that He would change His mind and shut the door, stopping me dead in my tracks? These questions can drive us mad, cause us to overanalyze the situation, and come to all kinds of conclusions that have no grounding in truth. I believe the more appropriate questions to ask would be: Where do I go after a door is closed? What can I learn from that experience?

The Theology of God's "Will" Versus His "Plan"

We can begin answering questions about things that happen to us by trying to understand an important distinction between human will and God's will. As far God's will for our life, that is easy: He wants us to live in righteousness. But, what takes more discernment and time is to know what God's *plan* is for our life. Let's take a look at the conflict of wills. In basic theology, we are exposed to the fact that man has been given a free will for a period of time. He is not a free moral agent who can act upon whatever impulses he wills. I know this may seem somewhat complex, but take a closer look at this concept with me. God is sovereign, meaning—He has supreme power and authority. But by His sovereign choosing, He allows man to act in opposition to His perfect will—*but not His ultimate plan.* Herein lies the tension between man's capacity to *will* his own life in one direction, and his ability to act on what he wills.

As I said, discovering God's will for your life is easy. There is no mystery there. Many in evangelical theology confuse God's "will" with His "plan," however. The will of God is an important biblical concept, but I have discovered that usually what people are trying to find when they talk about it is something different. The commandments and promises of God, which inform us what He requires us to do and believe are easy to find. God inspired men to write them in plain sight—in the Bible. If this is so, then what we are really looking to understand is not His will but rather His plan. Discovering His plan for us requires more discernment and intentional pursuit. Part of determining God's plan involves sincerely seeking God. When we do, we can discover what doors He desires to open and what doors He desires to close.

Let's put this principle into perspective. Imagine a time when an opportunity presented itself, and it looked absolutely appealing. Just because an opportunity looks and feels like the right thing for you doesn't necessarily mean it is from God, though. And likewise, just because an open door looks unappealing or somewhat uncertain doesn't mean you shouldn't walk through it. The key to finding your way in this dilemma then is knowing how to discern if an opportunity is really an open door that relates to God's divine plan. How will we know if His blessings and favor are attached to that path?

The Bible, God's revealed will, supplies us with some basic principles to assist us in discerning if an "open door" opportunity is a *God* idea or just a *good* idea. First, the door that God opens will never contradict His Word. God will never lead you toward any opportunity that would go against the rules He has given us about how to live our lives. Nor will He open a door that would require personal compromise or disobedience to His will in order for you to enter. Anything that contradicts the Word of God is a temptation, not an opportunity.

Second, the door that God opens will be accompanied by confirmation. God will often confirm an open door as an invitation from Him or prove it by supplying "the evidence of two or three witness" (2 Corinthians 13:1 ESV), whether they are verses from the Word of God, advice from someone seasoned in Scripture, or a noncompromising circumstance that continues to present itself.

Last, a door that God opens will be aligned with total dependence on Him. God will never give us an opportunity that will alienate us from Him or make us believe we no longer need Him. He is a God of relationships, a God who insists upon being first in our lives.

When A Door Closes, What is God Up To?

If you are like me, you have had situations in your life that you prayed about because you wanted them to work out. You may have even felt confident that you were interpreting God's will correctly. So you made your plans accordingly, only to discover the door had suddenly shut. Maybe it was a job opportunity that seemed promising, a relationship leading toward marriage, or relocation to another city or state. Whatever the situation, the initial reaction to that door closing on you is confusion, disappointment, and despair. It is at this point that we must rely on the infinite wisdom of God. God often uses closed doors to not only redirect us toward His perfect will, but also because He knows you won't move forward with His perfect plan unless your circumstances force you to move. But there is another element to consider when God closes a door in your life: Helen Keller, the famously deaf and blind author and humanitarian of the twentieth century, once wrote: "When one door of happiness closes, another opens, but often we look so long at the closed door we do not see the one that has opened for us." What a profound and very insightful statement coming from someone who was given severe challenges in early childhood.

The story of King David at the end of his life gives us another perfect example of how God opens one door as soon as He closes another.

In 1 Chronicles 17:1, David's thoughts turn to building a house for the Lord. The king sent for the prophet Nathan and said, "Here I am, living in a house of cedar, but the ark of God dwells in a tent" (2 Sam. 7:2; 1 Chron.17:1 ESV). A passion arises in David to construct a temple for the Lord—not for his own acclaim, but for the worship, honor, and glory of God. It's a noble idea, and the prophet Nathan even confirms his aspirations, saying, "Go, do all that is in your heart, for the LORD is with you" (2 Sam. 7:3; 1 Chron. 17:2 ESV). God's "will" is seemingly clear: David should erect a house dedicated to the Lord, so generation after generation could extol the God who had delivered them and now preserved them.

But don't miss the critical factor involved in this plan. This factor is why God closed the door on this well-intentioned good idea. The idea for the temple originated with David, not God. From the dialogue David has with the prophet Nathan, it is also clear that David may have felt guilty when he compared his magnificent palace with the humble tent. The fact still remains that God never asked David to build Him a temple, nor did He give David any instructions about how to do it. Compare David's temple project with the tabernacle of Moses. With the tabernacle project, not only did the idea originate with God, but God meticulously revealed every detail to Moses to allow him to be successful. So much so that, it takes over six and a half chapters to describe how it should be built (Exodus 25:1

> You weren't placed on the earth to stumble around in the dark trying to find out what you should do.

through 31:11). This confirms my original statement that God not only reveals His "will"—His general objective or desire for us—He also discloses His larger plan. This is the preordained design, the meticulous details regarding how to achieve or fulfill His will.

When you consider the conversation between David and Nathan, it would be natural for us to conclude that God would not only recognize his impulse as an attempt to honor Him, but that this impulse would be commended and allowed by the prophet. After David received the nod of approval from Nathan, he became obsessed and utterly consumed with the project. His emotional attachment to the project and plenary activity is documented 1 Chronicles chapter 29. He expressed: "I have set my affection on the house of my God" (1 Chron. 29:3 KJV). In the book of Psalm he prays:

> "Lord, remember David
> and all his afflictions;
> How he swore to the Lord,
> and vowed to the Mighty One of Jacob:
> "Surely I will not go into the chamber of my house,
> or go up to the comfort of my bed;
> I will not give sleep to my eyes
> or slumber to my eyelids,
> Until I find a place for the Lord,
> A dwelling place for the Mighty One of Jacob."
> (Psalm 132:1-5 NKJV)

If this Psalm is indeed talking about the construction of the temple (as "a dwelling place" indicates) and it is not hyperbole, then we have good reason to believe that David had insomnia during this time—something quite common for people suffering from an addiction to work. When we are sold on putting a good idea into action, sometimes we too can become obsessed with our desires and the planning process, to the point of compulsion. This is why when things don't work out quite how we intended or even when something we're working on completely shuts down, we have difficulty dealing with the disappointment.

David's obsession with his new project would soon be confronted with a reality check. Despite his good intentions and Nathan's commendation, God's plans for David were different. God denied him. God said that two-letter command we don't like hearing: no. "Thus says the LORD: It is not you who will build me a house to dwell in" (1 Chron. 17:4 ESV). The good intention in David's heart wasn't to be. It wasn't God's will for David to build the temple; rather, David prepared the way for the temple. We see this when David begins stockpiling materials and resources for the promised construction of God's house—a house he would never get to see (1 Chron. 22:2-5).

The blueprint was there, the plans were made, the materials were collected, but the building wouldn't be realized in David's day. This must have been perplexing for David. The man after God's own heart would never get to walk in God's house. As is always the case, His ways aren't our ways, nor His plans our plans. God promises to David that He would raise up his offspring, Solomon, who would usher in a reign of peace and prosperity. "When your days are fulfilled to walk with your fathers, I will raise up your offspring after you, one of your own sons, and I will establish his kingdom. He shall build a house for me, and I will establish his throne forever" (1 Chron. 17:11-12 ESV). He then commissions his son Solomon to "arise and work" (1 Chron. 22:16), for he was the one who was destined to see the Lord's house built in all its glory.

I can't help but think that these words aren't only intended to foreshadow what God would do through Solomon, but also what God would do through His own Son, Jesus Christ. He wasn't only going to raise up David's son, He was going to bring a Savior. Both would bring true, lasting peace and rest. The promised Messiah would come from "David's body" (2 Sam. 7:12). The true and better Son of David would come and establish God's Kingdom. David might have wanted to build God a house, but God's plan was better. He was going to build *David* a house. "Moreover, I declare to you that the LORD will build you a house" (1 Chron. 17:10 ESV). God makes a covenant with David—something much better than any construction project David could've pulled off. And so David passes away, denied a good thing but promised a better one. God closed one door but opened another.

Doors of opportunity will seem to open and close before us in life. Sometimes our disappointments in life can become God's appointments, so don't let closed doors bother you. The things we think of as failures or problems at the time can often end up being blessings in disguise. When you are open to following God's will, He will lead you through those "open" doors and away from and around those "closed" doors. Solomon, the son of King David, advised us saying: "Trust in the LORD with all your heart, and lean not on your own understanding; In all your ways acknowledge Him, And He shall direct your paths" (Proverbs 3:5-6 NKJV).

God will guide you if you'll trust Him. You weren't placed on the earth to stumble around in the dark, trying to find out what you should do on your own. If you're sure that you are operating in God's will and you're confronted with opposition then move along to the next door. Knowing and meditating on God's Word will teach you to recognize when you should abandon the plans you might have made for yourself. God will give you a peace that surpasses all human understanding in return for closing a door that was not His will for your life. God has a plan and path for you, but it's your responsibility to find and follow it.

PART II

UNDERSTANDING
THE GOD-AND-MAN
RELATIONSHIP

CHAPTER 7

PLAYING WITH FIRE

When you pass through the waters, I will be with you;
And through the rivers, they shall not overflow you.
When you walk through the fire, you shall not be burned,
Nor shall the flame scorch you.
                    –Isaiah 43:2 (NKJV)

WHEN GOD WAS ANGRY, A fire burned Israel (Isaiah 42:25), but now, with God on their side, they are invincible against even the most severe trials. Fire is a common metaphor for extreme peril. This may be because fire consumes all. Fire leaves nothing but ashes. God uses His fire either to purify and cleanse the believer (a blessing) or to bring judgment upon the sinner or one who transgresses against His will.

In Proverbs chapter six Solomon uses the analogy of burning oneself to describe sinning. He asks:

> "Can a man take fire to his bosom, and his clothes
> not be burned? Can one walk on hot coals, and his
> feet not be seared?"
>
> (Proverbs 6:27-28 NKJV)

If you say that someone is "playing with fire," you mean that they are doing something dangerous that may result in great harm to them or may cause many other problems. That turn of phrase is used as advice against taking a course of action that may result in an unpleasant outcome either for themselves or others around them.

When I was a teenager, for example, I was fascinated by the Bunsen burner that came with a chemistry set I was given one Christmas. For those who may not be familiar with what a Bunsen burner is, it is a piece of laboratory equipment that produces a single open gas flame, which is used for heating and sterilization. While I was always intrigued with the carefully designed experiments included in the booklet accompanying my student's chemistry set, I was also a curious and adventurous teen. My mother knew it, and her keen maternal instincts advised me to be careful. She knew the damage that particular gas-burning piece of equipment could inflict, so she warned me never to use it except carefully and during experiments. She would say with a cautious smile, "You know . . . if you play with fire, one day you will get burned."

Well, that one day came. I decided to give in to my adventurous nature. I attempted to invent my own fireworks. I researched the chemicals normally used in commercial fireworks, and began my independent experiment. I reasoned, "If I'm careful and follow the boundaries I've discovered through my research, as I did with my experiment cards, I should be fine."

My first mistake was conducting this rogue experiment in my bedroom. I should have gone out into the backyard, in the open air! I mixed the chemicals, set them to the side, and fired up the burner. Just then, my mother called me. I left the room to see what she wanted—without turning off the burner! My second mistake. As soon as I returned to the room, I could smell the fumes from the chemicals. In that moment, I realized what was about to happen. In an instant, there was a fizzing sound, and an odd smell filled my room. It began to seep out into the rest of the house. I opened my room door, but as I rushed to shut off the burner, my mixture began to spark. Then it exploded, shattering the bowl it was in and sending water, chemicals from my set, and glass everywhere.

With my heart beating fast, I laid down on my bedroom floor, near my window. I tried to gather my composure. I was certain my mother had heard the explosion, and I was even more certain that she would tell my dad! Suddenly, I saw my mother approaching. I was scared. I didn't want her to find out that I went off script, that I'd caused the explosion as a result of not using the chemistry set's instruction cards. I noticed my handwritten notes about my experiment lying out in plain sight, so I threw my legs over them to hide what I was attempting to concoct.

She entered my room, and her beautiful brown piercing eyes stretched wide in disbelief. Looking around and trying to make sense out of what just happened, she shouted at me with a frantic tone, "Move your legs! There's a fire underneath them!" I was unaware that the sparks from the explosion had ignited my notes, which were indeed smoldering. Fortunately, I moved my legs quickly enough that I did not get burned. After putting out my flaming notes, my mother made a few chastising remarks and told me clean up the mess my experiment had caused before my father got home.

> Playing with God is a very dangerous situation. It is playing with fire!

As I looked around my room, I realized I could have possibly burned up not only my room—I could have damaged a significant part of our home. It was then that I realized my mother's rule about not playing with fire was not meant to stifle my adventurous nature or to spoil my youthful fun, it was meant to keep me safe.

Sometimes we don't understand the reasons behind God's commands. We may even think He is a cosmic killjoy, setting up rules and regulations to keep us from enjoying ourselves. But God asks us to obey Him because He has our best interests at heart. So, when God warns us not to sin or not to make a particular decision, He does it for our own good. He really wants to protect us from "playing with fire" and getting burned.

Although my mother and I have had many laughs about that incident—and my many other teenage fun-filled unapproved adventures throughout the years—looking back now, I see that my ill-advised experiment could have caused my entire family a season of pain and confusion. While some fires can be destructive, the fire that God allows us to experience often provokes deep spiritual and psychological questions about our lives. Fire also provides opportunities for new growth. It is during such times of trial that we should turn our attention to His unfailing counsel. If we will allow God's Word to saturate our heart and mind, it will unleash a heart-transforming power that will burn away our defenses and bring radical change to our life!

Satan Playing with God

The Book of Job is a prime example. Satan challenges God not once, but twice. Why does this matter? Well, it kind of makes us wonder if we, too, should be questioning God. But the reality is that it is about much more than just suffering, or even God's justice. It is important to note that Job suffers because he is one of the best men, not because he is one of the worst. God confidently commends Job to Satan's face: "There is no one on earth like him; he is blameless and upright, a man who fears God and shuns evil" (Job 1:8 NIV). Satan then rejects God's opinion of Job's good character. He attempts to convince God that Job has a selfish motive. Notice the cynical reason Satan gives God for Job obeying and trusting Him (Job 1:9-10): "Does Job fear God for nothing?" Satan asks. Clearly, this is an insinuation that Job is simply out to get something from God. Satan taunts God––playing with fire. "Have you not put a hedge around him and his household and everything he has?" Satan argues. "You have blessed the work of his hands, so that his flocks and herds are spread throughout the land."

With God's permission, Satan grabs a handful of dirty tricks from his bag of ways to make men suffer. He flings them at Job, and the world caves in on this innocent man. Job's children are killed. His herds and property are either carried off by raiders or destroyed by natural disasters. His wife and close friends betray him. Yet, even during his darkest moments in his life, Job continues to recognize how big and how great God is.

After all these horrific tragedies, Satan is proven wrong. It wasn't that Job had to overcome a specific sin, but rather that he had to grow in understanding. During the midnight hour of his sufferings, Job had been tempted to conclude that God was unjust or unable to rule in the right way.

But I believe that Job must have remembered King David's affirmation:

> "For his anger endureth but a moment; in his favour is life: weeping may endure for a night, but joy cometh in the morning. And in my prosperity, I said, I shall never be moved. Lord, by thy favour thou hast made my mountain to stand strong: thou didst hide thy face, and I was troubled."
>
> (Psalm 30:5-7 KJV)

The daybreak of Job's spiritual testing finally came, and his painful nighttime experiences ceased. Job gained a deeper, clearer perception of his Creator. But this new awareness was only a by-product of the real purpose of Job's suffering: to test his faith and love. In this case, God needed to know something about Job, and Job needed to know something about himself and about God.

Satan was playing with God's multipurpose fire. For Satan, God's fire would prove to be an in-your-face judgment. God slapped Satan with a reality check. When he confronts God and His people, he will lose every time! For Job, God's fire would prove that suffering had been an expansive, faith-demonstrating opportunity. In Job's reality, God had grown much bigger. At the same time, Job had become smaller in his own eyes.

Job vindicated both himself and God by remaining faithful. Job proved that despite our inability to understand or discern God's presence and agenda during our darkest moments, He is always with us. More important, there is always a God-ordained outcome. Here's what Job concluded: "But he knoweth the way that I take: when he hath tried me, I shall come forth as gold" (Job 23:10 KJV).

Man Playing with God

It is very dangerous to play with God. It is playing with fire! Living while moving in and out of sin is very inadvisable. Despite how we act or what we might hope to accomplish for our own small ends, it is impossible to outwit God. When we use God or the Bible to justify what we want to do, we leave an impression designed to work to our advantage. But when we create diversions to try to get through difficult situations without facing them forthrightly, God is not fooled. Promises are made with perhaps good intentions but are not kept. Even worse, declarations are made in an attempt to negotiate a situation we are trying to avert. Games like this will ultimately cause issues in a person's relationship with God.

The extreme version of the above scenario is even more devastating. It is one thing to play games with God, but it is quite another to "play God." That is *truly* playing with fire! Satan fell out of God's favor because of pride that originated from his desire to be God instead of a servant of God. In our world today, Satan takes advantage of everyday scenarios to tempt us into thinking we know more than God. The unfortunate spirit of our current generation is one of noncompliance and rebellion. This is a spiritual conflict that is the direct product of a self-assertive spirit. Many people believe that they can simply do whatever they want to do. They want what they want, when they want it. They are not willing to wait for God to give it to them in His way and according to His time schedule.

The two prevailing issues confronting both the believer and the nonbelievers in our generation are: ignorance of God's word, and disregarding God as sovereign and Lord of all. Notice the Apostle Paul's address to the Church in Rome:

> "For the invisible things of him from the creation of the
> world are clearly seen, being understood by the things
> that are made, even his eternal power and Godhead; so
> that they are without excuse: Because that, when they
> knew God, they glorified him not as God, neither were

thankful; but became vain in their imaginations, and their foolish heart was darkened. Professing themselves to be wise, they became fools, And changed the glory of the uncorruptible God into an image made like to corruptible man, and to birds, and four-footed beasts, and creeping things. Wherefore God also gave them up to uncleanness through the lusts of their own hearts, to dishonour their own bodies between themselves: Who changed the truth of God into a lie, and worshipped and served the creature more than the Creator, who is blessed forever. Amen."

(Romans 1:20-25 KJV)

Choosing not to acknowledge God or His sovereignty in this world is destructive; it will only lead to chaos. When we assert ourselves on the platform of self-governance and self-righteousness—trying to get what we deem we are entitled to—our minds become oblivious to the grip of our defiance toward God. In such a state of mind, we are deceived into disregarding the reality of possible consequences for our actions.

C. S. Lewis's profound statement on the problem of "mere Christianity" and the arrogance of man is that the two are competitive by nature. This affects our relationship with God and is dangerously futile. He said:

> *In God you come up against something which is in every respect immeasurably superior to yourself. Unless you know God as that—and, therefore, know yourself as nothing in comparison—you do not know God at all. As long as you are proud you cannot know God. A proud man is always looking down on things and people: and, of course, as long as you are looking down, you cannot see something that is above you.* [1]

Pride is the most terrible of all the vices that can smuggle themselves into the center of our Christian life.

It is purely spiritual, subtle, and sometimes deadly. In the Book of Acts, Luke holds defiance under a microscope as he records the situation where a married couple attempted to finesse the Apostle Peter. They were unaware that their actions were not just against a man of God, but against God Himself. There was astounding generosity in the early days of the church. The scriptures record that, "From time to time those who owned lands or houses sold them, brought the money from the sales and it was distributed to anyone as he had need" (Acts 4:34-35 NIV). As a result, "There were no needy persons among them."

A man named Ananias and his wife, Sapphira, sold a piece of property, just as many others had done. However, this couple kept

> It is right for mankind to respect God. Be in awe of, worship, and obey Him. He knows everything about His creation—even secret things.

part of the money and, apparently eager to be applauded and honored in the church, pretended to surrender the full price of the sale to the apostles. Peter confronted the couple with their lie, asking, "How is it that Satan has so filled your heart that you have lied to the Holy Spirit and have kept for yourself some of the money you received for the land?" (Acts 5:3 NIV).

Why had they conspired to "test the Spirit of the Lord" (v. 9)? Ananias and Sapphira attempted to play a bluffing game with God. They not only supposed they could deceive the church, but also sought to trick the Holy Spirit! But God saw through their scheme and called their bluff. Before the day was over, the couple had paid the price of playing with God: they paid with their lives.

If I were to suggest that God played games with us, it would only be one game: Truth or Consequences. Many of us, when we read this story, found God's actions here too harsh and probably offensive. But that only reveals how ignorant we are about the severity of sin and, conversely, the holiness of God. We shouldn't ask the question, "Why did they die?" Instead we should wonder, "Why do we remain alive?" Yes, God is patient with us and slow to anger. But as R. C. Sproul says, "We forget rather quickly that God's patience is designed to lead us to repentance . . . we use this grace as an opportunity to become more bold in our sin."

No, not everyone who lies or transgresses against God's will gets struck down immediately for their sin. So, the question still remains: Why did Ananias and Sapphira? If you review the history of God and His relationship with man, you will identify with a couple of reasons for His actions. First, their deaths—like many throughout the Bible—serve as a warning. When God makes a mandate, He puts it on public physical display. We see this most often through the healing miracles, but it is equally true of judgment. God doesn't do this with everyone who lies to the Holy Spirit today. But that should not cover up the fact that this death is a picture of how God feels about people who do lie to Him. It is a glimpse of the future judgment of all who entertain the thought of testing God.

Second, Ananias and Sapphira had witnessed the activity of the Holy Spirit up close and personal. This should have increased their knowledge of the seriousness of such a sin. This couple had seen the mercy of God firsthand. The irony in this story is that Ananias's name in fact means, "God is merciful." They had likely witnessed the death of Christ! And yet despite being recipients of His great grace, they disregarded it for the praise of men.

Have you ever thought about this one question: Do you respect God? Let me be clear about what I'm asking . . . Do you think God is worthy of your sincere consideration, worship, and obedience? We must ever keep the following truth in mind—low views of Scripture do not lend themselves to high views of God. In a world that has become increasingly in need of direction, the Word of God provides just the message needed to deal with our sinful nature, to navigate us through the difficulties of life, and to get to know God and His will.

It is right for mankind to respect God. We should be in awe of, worship, and obey Him. He knows everything about His creation—even secret things. He knows about all the good and all the bad, and He will judge people for everything they do. So, do not take God and His "holy will" lightly!

CHAPTER 8

AN AFFAIR TO SURRENDER

For I feel a divine jealousy for you,
since I betrothed you to one husband,
to present you as a pure virgin to Christ.
– 2 Corinthians 11:2 (NIV)

You're cheating on God. If all you want is your own way, flirting
with the world every chance you get, you end up enemies of God and
his way. And do you suppose God doesn't care? The proverb has it that
"he's a fiercely jealous lover." And what he gives in love is far better
than anything else you'll find. It's common knowledge that "God goes
against the willful proud; God gives grace to the willing humble."
– James 4:4-6 (MSG)

IF YOU ARE A CHRISTIAN, then you are married to Jesus. You
are a part of the body of Christ, which is His bride, and you cheat
on Him when you love the world. We all know the devastating
effects a mistress can have on a marriage, but many times we do not
understand the spiritual devastation that happens when we claim to
love Jesus while embracing the world in our arms. It is called having
a spiritual affair, or spiritual adultery. It is being unfaithful to God.
It is having an undue fondness for the things of the world.

When a man marries, he is committing himself to a relationship
with one woman. The honorable man will be faithful to his wife.

Cheating is out of the question. Because he values her, he won't do some of the things he used to when he was a single man. His love and commitment to her will help him make choices that will honor their marriage and deepen their relationship.

> God deserves our full allegiance.

Similarly, our faith in and relationship with Christ leads believers into a love relationship with God and a life submitted to God. God knows the challenges that we face in living for Him. He knows that it can be a real struggle. He tells us in His Word:

> "I say this to you: Let the Holy Spirit lead you in each step. Then you will not please your sinful old selves. The things our old selves want to do are against what the Holy Spirit wants. The Holy Spirit does not agree with what our sinful old selves want. These two are against each other. So, you can't do what you want to do."
>
> (Galatians 5:16-17 NLV)

If we are honest with ourselves, we know there are times we don't feel like choosing what's right. The old ways, the old friends, they call out to us, and we're tempted to be unfaithful. But remember, God knows and cares. He has sent the Holy Spirit to help us, but He won't make our decisions for us. Ultimately, it comes down to us to choose the correct path. The material world, with its contrived and deceitful schemes of phony values, worthless pursuits, and unnatural affections, is designed to lure us away from a pure relationship with God. Spiritual adultery, then, is the forsaking of God's love and the embracing of the world's values and desires.

Can a Christian Stray from Faith in God and Still Be in a Relationship with Him?

So, what do you do when you're faced with something that conflicts with your relationship with God? It's helpful in those moments to pause and reflect. Look to God, and ask yourself if you really want to be unfaithful to Him. How could we be, after all He has done for us? The key theological question for our secular age is said well by Collin Hansen: "Does God get to be God? The answer, even for many self-described Christians, is 'No, only on our terms.' You'll see many young adults who grew up in evangelical churches try to argue that unless we recast biblical and historical notions of God, we'll lose the next generations." [1] In other words, God's nature doesn't change to accommodate the values of modern secular society. It's on us to act in a way that honors His Word, regardless of whether or not that seems convenient in this day and age.

Choose to love Him more than whatever it is that's luring you away. Act on His promise: "No temptation has overtaken you except what is common to mankind. And God is faithful; he will not let you be tempted beyond what you can bear. But when you are tempted, he will also provide a way out so that you can endure it." (1 Corinthians 10:13 NIV) Look for that way of escape and run for it!

God deserves our full allegiance. He made a blood covenant with us through Jesus Christ. Our relationship with the world changed when we were reconciled with God. Nothing in our lives or culture should be more important to us than our relationship with Him. Jesus said, "No one can serve two masters. Either you will hate the one and love the other, or you will be devoted to the one and despise the other" (Matthew 6:24 NIV). The Bible exhorts us, "Do not love the world or anything in the world. If anyone loves the world, love for the Father is not in them. For everything in the world—the lust of the flesh, the lust of the eyes, and the pride of life—comes not from the Father but from the world. The world and its desires pass away, but whoever does the will of God lives forever" (1 John 2:15-16 NIV).

Some individuals mistakenly believe that as long as they give God *something*, they don't have to give God *everything*. And by extension, the pattern of their need to pretend to be faithful extends to their relationships in the body of Christ. They will pretend to be who they really are not, or will boast about things they never actually accomplished, deceiving members of the body of Christ. The problem is this: you may impress the body of Christ with your deception, but you will never deceive the Christ of the body.

We Are Either Faithful or Unfaithful to God, There Is No In-Between

I have been involved in premarital and marriage counseling for over twenty years. To better understand spiritual infidelity, let's look at a more familiar parallel: infidelity in marriage. Each type of infidelity has its own unique causes, and each needs to be dealt with in a different manner, but the core question is the same for both. What leads people to stray? What I have discovered is that there are three main ingredients that are present when people have an affair. These ingredients have a direct correlation to the spiritual infidelity that takes place in the Christian experience.

First, when affairs begin, a person falls in love with a fantasy. In our mind, we focus only on the other person's attractive qualities. In essence, we construct a fictional partner who will meet a desire that seems elusive in our current situation. The parallel situation for the Christian experience, is that we create a fantasy presented by the world to fill in an area in life where we feel somehow unsatisfied. In Matthew 13:18-23 Jesus shares a parable about the sower of seeds. Although He uses a metaphor of the fertility of the soil that the Word of God falls on, He's introducing us to the challenges of resisting worldly temptations that cause us to contemplate straying from our faithfulness to God. He summarizes the lure of the world: "the cares of this world, and the deceitfulness of riches, and the lusts of other things entering in, Jesus says they, choke the word, and it becomes unfruitful in our life" (Matthew 13:19 ESV). This opens us up to the fantasy of a worldly alternative path to personal fulfillment.

Worldly temptations are most dangerous enemies to a believer who is in a sincere relationship with God. The initial phase of spiritual infidelity transpires in a basic arc. We are drawn to the world's ways, as they appeal to our own sinful nature that longs to be

Arc of Spiritual Infidelity

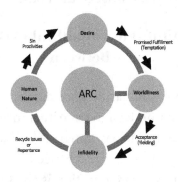

satisfied. Worldliness thrives in the culture of lies and deception. The world promises to fulfill your desires for sensual pleasure, material possessions, and instant gratification. The problem is, our personal desires and passions for worldly things *can't* be satisfied. Even if every desire was granted, we would always want more. Only through the power of God's Spirit are believers strengthened and equipped to control their passions. We must get past the desire for worldly goods in order to grow into a deeper love relationship with God.

Secondly, affairs are about an innate desire for external validation. Many individuals are not actually "falling in love" with another person, they are falling "in love" with a new image of themselves they fabricate in order to convince themselves they're still attractive. It is alluring and addictive to refashion ourselves this way, because the "new" person receives praise and external validation on a whole new level. The Christian self-image should be the most empowering element of our relationship with God. It is how you now see yourself in your new life through Christ, and is much more important than how other people see you. This is important, because it affects your self-esteem and gives you confidence in ways that are very different from the confidence we get by accumulating worldly markers of success. Apostle Paul reminds us of how important our confidence is and about who you are in God. The writer simply says, "So do not throw away your confidence; which has a great reward" (Hebrews 10:35 ESV).

During our lifelong walk with God, problems will arise that will challenge and sometimes even distort our confidence in our capacity to overcome. These affect us emotionally. They can compromise our self-confidence and make us seek the approval of other Christians. We want to receive validation from others who share our faith in God. When they disappoint us time after time, we begin to lose sight of God's acceptance. Unfortunately, at times even the body of Christ falls prey to secular values and judges a fellow believer according to their spiritual gifts, their personality, their likeability factor, their racial or cultural background, their socioeconomic status, and, yes, even their choices on open-ended issues—but we shouldn't. We should judge them according to the ways Christ validates good character.

When people don't feel like they're being evaluated on "Christlike" conditions, they often struggle with insecurity. The societal pressure to conform to the expectation of others rather than the expectations of God is immense, because our peers judge us instantly and often. The process and plan to lure the vulnerable Christian into the world's ideology and to generate a false sense of self begins. It stirs the longing to reimagine ourselves in a way that will gain man's approval. It is at this moment, however, that the spiritual influences over this world detect an open door into your relationship with God.

The Bible clearly states that, "The LORD does not look at the things people look at. People look at the outward appearance, but the LORD looks at the heart" (1 Samuel 16:7 NIV). While God's view of us is what should matter, the vulnerable Christian at this point is so in need of validation, he or she will buy into the world's view of things that will earn us acceptance. We become obsessed with improving physical appearance, financial status, levels of education, etc. Please understand, I agree that these areas of our life should be managed and improved within reason, but don't overlook the key word I used above: *obsessed*. Spiritual affairs begin when you "fall in love" with a new "outward image" rather than the "God image." We can't love both God and the world. Our hearts are complex and quite vulnerable. Because of them, we are drawn toward what we really want in life. The love for the world is birthed out of an appetite for pleasure—that's just human nature. A love for God is born out of the Spirit of God, for God's pleasure. James states it clearly, "But EVERY man is tempted, when he is drawn away of his OWN lust, and enticed" (James 1:14 KJV).

> Worldliness is one of the most dangerous traps for a believer.

Lastly, affairs are appealing because we get a feeling of intoxication with each new encounter. We get hooked on positive external feedback. It becomes addictive, and we quickly develop a need for more and more. This point is the sequel to the second reasons affairs begin. An outward image might garner man's approval, but the inward image is what God is most interested in. We live in a world where the common definition of self-esteem is feelings of worth based on skills, accomplishments, status, financial resources, or even appearance. This kind of self-esteem can lead a person to feel independent and prideful, and to indulge in self-worship, which dulls our desire for God.

When you become addicted to a need for outside approval, you learn to value the beliefs, opinions, and desires of others above your own. Their opinion of you will seem far more important than God's opinion of you. It is at this point that your entire decision-making system will be taken over by your need to earn approval. You will sacrifice God's dreams and future for your life in order to get that next new emotional fix—that next injection of compliments—the next external positive feedback. It is as if God's approval doesn't matter anymore, because it doesn't appeal to our carnal desires. In our carnality, we desire to be accepted. We want to matter to other people. Rejection hurts. Part of the reason rejection hurts so much is because it tears away from us the approval of mankind. If we can fight the urge to comfort ourselves by desperately seeking more human affirmation, we can use that hurt as an opportunity to surrender our affair with worldly desires and seek affirmation from God instead.

Concluding Thoughts to the Body of Christ: Spiritual Infidelity Is Also Triggered by Conscious and Subconscious Conflicts Within the Church

The Church of the Lord Jesus Christ was called to be steady, steadfast, and unmovable. She was called to be a light in the darkness. But our generation is preoccupied with compulsivity. We are allowing some issues to creep into the church that could cause harm to the souls entrusted to us. People who exhibit compulsive behaviors before entering a relationship with God tend to transfer those same behaviors into the church environment. In psychology, compulsive behaviors are explained as a coping mechanism designed to alleviate conscious, intense "psychic pain," anxiety, or unhappiness. Spiritual infidelity has a compulsive component to it too—without surrendering to the Spirit of God, the individual can't resist their inner urges.

I grew up in the Church. I have given my entire adult life to the calling and vocation of the ministry of the Gospel of Christ. One thing I have

> The reputation of God is in the hands of His Church. Beware! People tend to connect conflict in the church environment with God.

noticed in my almost forty years of ministry is that even Church people can really be cruel and mean-spirited when they are mad. They can cut you off, cut you up, and cut you out. It is sad to admit. But it is true. If we as the Body of Christ aren't careful, we will deter others from wanting to know the God we represent in this world. As children of God, we are called to first represent the Kingdom of God on the earth. Secondly, we are commissioned to preserve the reputation of God in deeds. The questions we must ask ourselves are: Are *we* dissuading the searching nonbeliever from coming to us to consider and learn about our God? Are we pushing individuals who already have a relationship with God back into the arms of the world (another lover) because of our behavior?

In James 4:1-12, he confronts the problem of conflicts within the church that could discredit the reputation of God and weaken the Church's influence in the world. We might have a romanticized image of the early church, but the followers to whom James wrote were at war with each other. Similar to our churches today, there was jealousy and selfish ambition (James 3:14, 16). Members were angrily quarreling with each other. As James points out, the source of their conflicts was selfishness. He tells us that resolving conflicts depends on repenting for selfish ways and humbling yourself before God.

Today, people tend to connect conflict in the church environment with God. People begin to become saddened in the sanctuary and depleted of hope even in the presence of God. How is this possible? It is because life with the people of God has become painful. The inability to find peace drives individuals to seek comfort by creating conflict even within the church by giving in to ungodly worldly concerns. It seems extremely difficult in this world to achieve the kind of unity, love, and concern for one another that Jesus Christ shared with His disciples. But as children of God, we must take a stand against the influences in this world that threaten the love covenant between us, our God, and each other. Our relationship with God should never be burdensome. Just like in a marriage, if God, as our partner, is not the ultimate desire of our heart, our relationship with Him will be in danger and our relationship will crumble.

We all must take intentional steps to improve our relationships with other members of God's Kingdom. Maybe you need to break up with some "false gods" in your life. Perhaps there are some desires, people, or things that are crippling your relationship with God. No, the grass is not greener on the other side of spiritual fence. That is only an illusion that will eventually reveal itself as a delusion. The only possible outcome of letting your relationship with God fall apart is a broken heart and a move away from God. Only the true God can fill the desires of your heart. Only God can completely fill the emptiness of your soul and grant you meaning and significance in this life.

In Revelation 2:1-7, Jesus sends a message to the church in Ephesus. He calls for the people of God to return to their "first love." Ephesus posed some unique challenges for Christ's early followers, because it was home to the Emperor's cult and was a place where people worshipped the Greek goddess Artemis (see: Acts 19:23-40). Because of these influences, the Ephesian believers had developed great discernment when it came to false teachers and heresy. Christ commended them for this discernment, but He still faulted them for having moved away their "first love." So, like the church in Ephesus then, there is a problem among believers today. As Doctor Tony Evans appropriately describes it, we are dealing with the cancer of carnality: "The first lover-stealer is the spiritual condition the New Testament calls carnality. Whether it's in our individual lives, our family life, our church life, or our life in society, a lot of what is wrong with us is attributable to our own carnality." He goes on to say, "God has too many children who are not really sure whose family they want to be a part of." [2]

Once you become indifferent to someone or something, the intensity of your passion for them diminishes. Acts of love become routine, without connection—life becomes mundane, devoid of any meaningful purpose. The "first love" that characterized the Church at Ephesus was the zeal and ardor with which they embraced their salvation as they realized they loved Christ because He first loved them (1 John 4:19). It was, in fact, His love for them that had made them "alive together with Christ." But they gradually lost their warmth and zeal for Christ. When that happened, they began to "go through the motions" of doing good works, motivated not by the love of Christ, but by the works themselves. What was once a love relationship cooled into mere routine. Their passion for Him became little more than a cold adherence to orthodoxy.

Instead of pursuing Christ with the devotion they once showed, much like a bride who would follow her groom "through the desert" (Jeremiah 2:2), the Ephesians were in danger of falling away from

Christ completely. This is why He warns those who have "ears to hear" (Revelation 2:7) to prove the reality of their salvation by returning to Him and rekindling the love that had begun to cool. He warns the rest not to follow them, but to repent and return to Him with the passion they once had for Him.

We are faced with the same challenges in the twenty-first century. Stop opposing God. Stop avoiding Him. Surrender your affair with human desires and worldly influences—they will only lead to life complications and eventually severe consequences. Renew your vows with God and devote yourself to Him in every way. Take the time to look at the ways you are cheating on Him, and do everything you can to resist Satan as we are urged to do in James 4:7. Are you willing to do this for a God who loves you more than anything? A God who, even while you were cheating on Him, sent His only Son to take your sin away just so He could have a relationship with you? A God who was willing to die for you when you were only looking out for yourself (Romans 5:8-10)?

When you consider all He has done on our behalf, do you really still believe that God is unreasonable to ask that we surrender the totality of our "selves" to Him? Is there any downside to *not* surrendering? Well, if you do not surrender, you leave the safety of His will for the uncertainty of your own. It is worth pondering.

CHAPTER 9

PRIDE AND PREJUDICE

He spoke this parable to some who trusted in
themselves that they were righteous,
and despised others: "Two men went up to the temple to pray, one a
Pharisee and the other a tax collector. The Pharisee stood and prayed
thus with himself, 'God, I thank You that I am not like other men—
extortioners, unjust, adulterers, or even as this tax collector. I fast
twice a week; I give tithes of all that I possess.' And the tax collector,
standing afar off, would not so much as raise his eyes to heaven,
but beat his breast, saying, 'God, be merciful to me a sinner!
– Luke 18:9-13 (NKJV)

THIS CHAPTER TITLE WAS INSPIRED by Jane Austen's 1813 novel *Pride and Prejudice*. I remember reading the novel in college for an English literature second-year class. Although this classic novel is not the focus of chapter nine, it speaks to the basic theme. The story chronicles the emotional development of the central character, Elizabeth Bennet, the daughter of a country gentleman, and Fitzwilliam Darcy, a rich and aristocratic landowner.

Although these two main characters are intrigued by each other from the start, Austen reverses the convention of first impressions: "pride" of rank and fortune and "prejudice" against Elizabeth's inferior family tree render Darcy indifferent, proud, and unapproachable. It is a classic tale about the trials and tribulations of falling in love despite the complications of social classes. Besides the obvious themes of love and self-understanding, there is a Christian message hidden in this story as well, about the transformational power of love.

Our love relationship with God and how we, as believers, represent Him to each other as well as to an unrighteous world is stunningly similar to the struggle found in both the Book of Luke and the novel *Pride and Prejudice*. When you look at these stories, you will find different angles, and various

> Pride is often cast as the most selfish of the deadly sins.

plot shadings, but the struggle at the heart of the love story is still the same, just rendered in different ways. One predominant common thread weaves itself through the tapestry of both stories: pride. Various scriptures depict God's position on pride. We will discuss these further later in this chapter.

To understand pride, we must understand the nature of prejudice. Prejudices are related to prejudgments. Gordon Allport, an American psychologist, who focused his studies on personality psychology, stated that, "Prejudgments become prejudices only if they are not reversible when exposed to new knowledge." He argues that we emotionally resist evidence that contradicts our prejudices, unlike what happens with ordinary prejudgments. Thus, we have another ingredient of prejudice: resistance to new knowledge.[1] Our relationship with God and others is dependent on the principle of "knowing," which of course relates to gathering knowledge. This doesn't mean just amassing facts, but also by striving for proper *understanding*.

King Solomon enlightened us to this truth. He says, "The fear of the Lord is the beginning of wisdom, and knowledge of the Holy One is understanding" (Proverbs 9:10 NIV). Paul the Apostle also admonishes us to "not conform to the pattern of this world, but be transformed by the renewing of your mind. Then you will be able to test and approve what God's will is—his good, pleasing and perfect will" (Romans 12:2 NIV). God's position on pride and prejudice is this: "Pride goeth before destruction, a haughty spirit before a fall" (Proverbs 16:18 KJV). The wisest king of all time makes it absolutely clear that God has a serious problem with pride, which can also be defined as an erroneous belief in our own knowledge, and its pal, prejudice. If they are a serious issue for God, then they should be a serious issue for us as well.

Pride in Context

Pride is one of the classic seven deadly sins. And it is the most dangerous of all sins, in a sense, because pride is the one sin against which there is no certain defense. I can try to resist greed or gluttony. I can work on my feelings of envy or anger. I can fight off the pull of idleness and desire. But pride is immune to such efforts. In fact, the more accomplished you get even at resisting temptation, the more a sinful sense of pride can blossom out of our success at doing something holy!

So, what is pride? Is it really a deadly sin, or could it be a virtue? Well, that depends. Don't be shocked by my statement. Take a closer look at it with me, and I will explain. You've surely heard someone say: "Take pride in a job well done," or "Take pride in what you do." Those are well-intentioned statements meant to encourage us to do our best. Then we have Solomon stating that: "Pride goeth before destruction, a haughty spirit before a fall," (Proverbs 16:18 KJV). In the book of Job the author penned: "There they cry out, but He does not answer, because of the pride of evil men" (Job 35:12 NKJV). When the Bible warns us about pride, it's not talking about the sense of delight that comes when you complete a project or see your children accomplish something wonderful. But I will issue a word of warning as we explore the context of pride. Healthy, humble delight in accomplishments can easily morph into unhealthy, arrogant overvaluing of oneself.

I want to dissect this concept further by pointing out that there are two kinds of pride. On the one hand, we have that kind of pride that is arrogant, conceited, and narcissistic; on the other hand, we have a humbler pride, one that follows proportionately with success. The first kind is what psychologists call *excessive* pride; the second, *authentic* pride. Deciding whether pride is a deadly sin or a virtue depends on the very kind of pride, excessive or authentic, that one is talking about.

One of the most interesting facets of these two kinds of pride is the impact each has on prejudice. Pride is often cast as the most selfish of the deadly sins, and indeed, excessive pride is a self-absorbed, other-shunning emotion that can only increase the spirit of prejudice. However, authentic pride, generated in proportion to actual worthy accomplishments, leaves room for the concerns of others and, as a result, may *decrease* the influence of prejudice. Individuals who allow the spirit of excessive pride to control their relationships consciously target those they consider as "outgroups" (e.g., other races, cultures, religions, educational levels). They even target individuals at different spiritual maturity levels and in different types of family groups. The list can go on and on, but I think you understand the gist of where the prejudice of excessive pride can lead.

Jesus dealt with pride and prejudice in the parable found in the book Luke. He exposed those who trusted in their own righteousness but treated others with contempt. Jesus looks right into the eyes of the people who are supposedly religious, realizing they do not understand the depth of what He just said concerning the publican and the tax collector. Waiting with baited breath for Him to continue, He makes this challenging controversial statement: "This tax man, not the other, went home made right with God. If you walk around with your nose in the air, you're going to end up flat on your face, but if you're content to be simply yourself, you will become more than yourself" (Luke 18:14 MSG).

The religious leaders of Jesus's time talk endlessly *about* God, but they did not know how to be right *with* God. They didn't know how to be right with others. I'm

> Pride causes us to filter out the evil we see in ourselves, it also causes us to filter out the goodness of God in others.

afraid that this same ideology has trickled down from the first-century church into the twenty-first century church. With regret, I have witnessed throughout my ministry churches and church people who do not know how to let go of their comfortable traditions and pious prejudices to fear God and do what is right.

Authentic pride is something to be praised, but excessive pride—or should I say spiritual pride—leads to ungodly prejudice, and that is something to be purged! We must come to

> Pride can cause us to hold others in contempt without any rational basis.

terms with our affair with self-righteousness and surrender to God. Spiritual pride is something that all believers will want to be careful to guard against. Perhaps it is true that there is a "little Pharisee" in each of us, manifesting our own self-righteousness in various ways. The way God treats spiritual pride should give all believers reason to be extra wary of the sin. Consider the thoughts in Proverbs alone:

"The fear of the Lord is to hate evil;
Pride and arrogance and the evil way
And the perverted mouth, I hate."
(Prov. 8:13 NKJV)

Pride in the Church

Throughout history, pride has been recognized as the deadliest of vices. Today, it is now almost celebrated as a *virtue* in our culture. Pride and arrogance are conspicuous among the rich, the powerful, the successful, the famous, and even some religious leaders. But make no mistake, it is also alive and well in ordinary people, including Christians. Yet few of us realize how dangerous it is to our souls, and how greatly it hinders our intimacy with God and our ability to love others in the body of Christ. Humility, on the other hand, is often seen as *weakness*, and few of us know much about it or even pursue it. For the good of our souls, then, we need to gain a clearer understanding of pride and humility and of how to forsake the one and embrace the other.

Religious pride often strikes close to home for true believers. If we are inclined to say to ourselves, "Lord, I thank you that I am not like that proud Pharisee," we should bear in mind that the apostles themselves were infected with pride. They bickered with one another about who was the greatest (Luke 22:24-27). Sadly, self-promotion in pursuit of reputation, influence, and "success," is evident in our churches even today. But if the apostles had to struggle with it, who are we to think ourselves exempt?

Spiritual pride takes many forms and shapes, and can wrap the heart like the layers of an onion: when you pull off one, there is another underneath. The biblical perspective on pride can be summarized as an attitude of self-sufficiency, self-importance, and self-exaltation in relation to God. Pride causes us to conveniently filter out seeing the evil in ourselves; it also causes us to filter out seeing the goodness of God in others. When we are prideful, we sift through our impressions of other people, letting only their faults pass through. This is the main door by which the devil comes into the hearts of those who are zealous for the advancement of Christ.

Spiritual Pride and the Prejudice of Others

When pride is directed toward others, it comes across as an attitude of contempt and indifference. It is a spiritual cancer that eats up every possibility of love, contentment, or even common sense. Pride crouches down, then pounces on the struggles of others. It encourages us to belittle others to aggrandize ourselves. The form it takes may vary from one person to the next, and it can be obvious or concealed. Spiritual pride asserts itself with a certain self-confident boldness before God and men. It causes a person to assume much about themselves, so it treats others with neglect. Pride prefers some people over others. It often clings to those who the world deems worthy of honor, giving more weight to their words, their wants, and their needs. We consciously or subconsciously pass over the fragile, the undesirable, and the unattractive, because they don't seem to offer us much.

Within the Church, an environment of pride can lift our

estimation of ourselves for no good reason. Pride can cause us to hold others in contempt without any rational basis. It is a dividing force. This makes it a lethal weapon Satan uses to destroy our testimony, shut down the witness of the church to others, and repel the interest of seekers who have a desire to know God. Jesus even experienced how belittling "religious" people can be. All four Gospels and Acts tell how Jesus hailed from Nazareth, but historically, that was an undesirable place to come from and others mocked Him for it.

While Jesus was turning the world upside down and impacting multitudes with the Gospel of the Kingdom of God, some self-righteous people did not share in the enthusiasm and anticipation of Jesus's coming. In the Gospel of John chapter one, we read about many witnesses. Everyone is testifying. But as we come to the end of the first chapter, we meet another type of witness—Nathaniel.

It is important to note Nathaniel's attitude in this passage, because it is still common among believers today. Philip claims: "We have found Him of whom Moses in the law, and also the prophets, wrote—Jesus of Nazareth, the son of Joseph" (John 1:44*b* NKJV). Unfortunately, Nathaniel's first reaction to this news is rather disappointing. Nathaniel actually mocks Jesus with his response: "Can anything good come out of Nazareth?"

We might miss the importance of that line, because Jesus quickly turns everything around a few verses later. But what did it mean? What is all this about Nazareth? Simply put, being from Jerusalem was good, being from Nazareth was bad. Nathaniel was *discriminating* against Jesus. Jesus had to work to convince Nathaniel to step outside of the prejudice informed by his pride. He had to convince him to make an effort to listen instead of defining Him based on His place of origin. This was a critical moment for Nathaniel. His pride and prejudice almost made him miss the revelation of the long-awaited Messiah who was revealed in the form of a man from Nazareth.

That was Jesus. Imagine what any one of us would do. Why do people look down on others? Especially those of us who say we are children of God? Why do people need to feel superior to others, or feel the need to put others down in order to feel better themselves?

Whether it is pride, insecurity, or prejudice, it is all rooted deeply in the imperfection that has been affecting humanity ever since the first couple in the Garden of Eden decided to stop obeying the guidance of their creator—God. Pride makes us adopt self-serving biases. To the extent that we "construct" reality, then, we construct it to serve an inflated view of ourselves over others—exactly what we would expect if we accept the biblical notion of fallen human nature. [2]

Spiritual Pride and Your Identity

Since the fall of man, the wheel of disobedience has continued to turn and turn. And with the fickle turning of that wheel, the irrational prides in our hearts are tempted to fall prey to its lure. Most people, knowingly or not, imitate the attitudes of the devil, not God. For this reason, pride and hatred are so much a part of our everyday life that we barely even notice them anymore. Here is the challenge for us today in an "unreasonable" world: a return to a faith beyond the boundaries of our fears, the shadow of our hatreds, and the limitations of our pride.

Pride can blur your authentic identity, as found in God through Christ Jesus. To believe the lie that is espoused by pride is to fall prey to the devil's trap of illusion. He seeks to confuse, and then ultimately to deceive. Could it be that more of us struggle with pride than we thought? Are we what we were, or are we who we are? If you are tempted to compare yourself with others, the questions may differ. Am I them, or am I me? Do I round everything off to the nearest stereotype? Do I strive to see people for who they are, rather than who I expect them to be? Pride can be an issue for us all, but there's good news for the prideful: a confession of pride signals the beginning of the end for pride. It indicates the war is already being waged. For only when the Spirit of God is moving, already humbling us, can we remove the lenses of pride from our eyes and see ourselves clearly, identifying the illness and seeking a cure.

Even as light can grow from darkness, so too can righteous love, mutuality, and true humility burst forth once again. We need only to look to what is inside our hearts and minds and souls. Look there, inside ourselves. Allow the Spirit of God to open our spiritual eyes to look and then to undertake a solemn duty to transform what we find into something worthy for the times we face ahead and worthy of the relationships we hold sacred with God and with each other. And with God's grace, we should turn daily to the Word of God, which can help us identify our sources of pride in all their hiding places inside of us. Let us pray with David:

> "Search me, O God, and know my heart!
> Try me and know my thoughts!
> And see if there be any grievous way in me,
> and lead me in the way everlasting!"
> (Psalm 139:23-24 ESV)

CHAPTER 10

INCONVENIENT
CHRISTIANITY

The Church is herself only when she exists for humanity . . .
She must take her part in the social life of the world, not
lording [her role] over men, but helping and serving them.
She must tell men, whatever their calling, what it means
to live in Christ, to exist for others.
– Dietrich Bonhoeffer, *Letters and Papers from Prison*

A TRUE CHRISTIAN CAN BE defined by both faith and action. "Therefore, if anyone is in Christ, he is a new creation. The old has passed away; behold, the new has come" (2 Corinthians 5:17 ESV). James says, "I will show you my faith by my works" (James 2:18 ESV). Jesus put it this way: "I am the light of the world. Whoever follows me will not walk in darkness, but will have the light of life" (John 8:12 ESV). A true Christian will show his faith by how he lives.

Despite the wide variety of beliefs that fall under the general "Christian" label today, the Bible defines a true Christian as one who has personally received Jesus Christ as Savior, who trusts in the death and resurrection of Jesus Christ alone for

> One of the reasons Christianity is overlooked is because it is so annoying to our convenient lifestyle.

forgiveness of sins, who has the Holy Spirit residing within, and whose life corroborates change consistent with faith in Jesus.

I must warn you up front that to corroborate a life consistent with Jesus's is to live a life of inconvenience. It is imperative that I clarify this. Christianity is *not*, in essence, just a moral code or an ascetic routine, as so many down the centuries have mistakenly supposed. Rather, it is super-naturalizing a personal relationship with a supernatural personal Savior for the purpose of a supernatural assignment. "We the people of God" are mandated to become disciples—persons, that is, who conscientiously, as our life project, walk with Him, learn from Him, worship Him and God the Father through Him. We maintain obedience to Him, conform ourselves to His recorded attitudes and example up to the limit of the Holy Spirit's enabling.

Pleasing God Will Interrupt Your Life

If you are willing to be made uncomfortable in the cause of a real and deep personal renewal, hopefully this chapter will challenge, humble, and inspire you. As authentic Christians, we are tasked with the responsibility of healing those who are discontent with a low view of Christianity. We must rise above a stunted "Jesus-and-me" faith and reclaim God's holy vision for His church.

To do so, it is our duty to confront one of the most prevailing issues of our day: the inconvenience of Christianity. I became a Christian at the tender age of twelve, and I will be turning sixty years old this year. One thing I have discovered as certain during my walk with God is that, like Christ, our efforts to please Him will interrupt our life when it is most inconvenient! It's not just that it seems inconvenient to befriend God, it is also a demanding challenge to walk through life with Him. Yes, it truly is! But here is a fact, and there is no getting around it: there is a cost to honoring God, and it is counted in the currency of convenience. The good news is that the cost pales in comparison to the purchase price of the great rewards that belong to a true disciple of Christ. Present and future blessings will come to the faithful Christian.

I recently came across an amazing book entitled *I Wish Jesus Hadn't Said That.* It is a wonderful short read that addresses ten of Jesus's hard and difficult sayings. The author chose them because they are difficult words to obey and live out. The book explains how radical the call to discipleship can be, and explains that it can only be achieved through the power of the Gospel, by living moment to moment under the Lordship of Jesus.[1] We need both the power of the Gospel and a submitted life to Christ, because only those who deny themselves are capable of living the inconvenient Christian life.

As Christians, we often have a very different perspective on life from those around us. This extends to how we view what every new experience means. The average Christian believes that unwanted challenges are forced upon us, which can make us feel like God did not give us time to agree with the prescribed challenges we now face that He has allowed to come into our life. The reality is much simpler than we realized and is, unfortunately, absolutely unimaginable for most of us. It is plainly stated in the Bi-ble that, as His children, we are required to "take up our cross and follow Christ" (Matthew 16:24). That is, we all should have a reasonable expectation of a challenging life, yet very few of us want to acknowledge that the cross was symbolic of a burden for *us* to carry, a responsibility to fulfill, and a convenience to forfeit. We usually remain stuck on the "finished work of the cross," and the "victory beyond the cross," but somehow, in our humanness, we tend to overlook the fact that the cross also means pain and inconvenience.

One of the reasons we gloss over the inconvenience of the cross is simply because it is so annoying. The two greatest problems in the world are *sin* in the body and *self* in the soul. These two issues are bound to the world. They create a two-strand stronghold cord that binds us and keeps us from fulfilling God's assignment through us to humanity. Only when we cut self from the strands that bind us (symbolically, through a mind transformation that stems from adherence to the Word of God) will we be released to cooperate with the inconvenient elements of the cross we must bear and the plan of God we may disagree with.

As idealistic as it may sound, if we want to capture the essence of true Christianity and the true image of God, we must see inconveniences like God sees them. In God's eyes, they are opportunities rather than annoyances. When personal inconvenience is the framework of your willingness to work for humanity, the character and love of Christ shines that much brighter through you. So, what *does* God have to say about your inconvenient Christianity? *Just do it!*

As a senior pastor, I have continually been impressed by the people who come forward ready to serve in areas of need. I have always been an advocate for serving God's agenda with your spiritual gifts as well as your natural talents. We will all be faced with tasks that should be completed even though you may not want to do them. We will all be challenged to deal with the uncertainty of life's many issues when things come up out of nowhere. These are the moments when we can make a great impact for the kingdom through our love expressed in "inconvenient" acts of kindness and care. After all, "inconvenience" is an opportunity for spiritual growth.

The Cost of Christianity

The Bible teaches us that God wants us to count the cost of our commitment to Him, because He knows it will demand everything we have. In Luke 14:28, Jesus paints a vivid picture of the cost factor involved in doing God's will as a disciple. He warns us away from a rosy view of following Him. I have experienced this dilemma time and again in the body of Christ that is our church throughout my ministry—an individual's enthusiasm withers when they start out with a romanticized view of what it means to be a Christian, when their commitment becomes inconvenient, or when it collides with the full cost of bearing the cross of Christian service.

We must give up the idea that there will be bits and pieces of our lives that can remain unaffected by our relationship with God through Christ Jesus. We can't say "yes" to God and still expect to hold on to a portion of our independence. He demands all of us. We no longer have the choice to serve only when and where it is convenient for us either. Our assignment as a disciple will take us to some strange and unexpected places that require dedication and He will ask us to carry heavy responsibilities.

God's Son was not exempted from this inconvenience. When you consider Jesus, no one was more inconvenienced than He! He came from an eternal and infinite blissful existence, laid aside His divine privileges, and inconveniently became a human—for humanity. And even though He was on a mission to fulfill His destiny of redeeming all mankind by His sacrificial death on the cross, He was consistently interrupted with what was seen by His disciples on many occasions as the most inconvenient requests at the most inconvenient times.

Luke records a series of these interruptions. In 8:41, Jesus was in a crowd when He was implored by a man named Jairus to come heal his daughter. While on His way to that assignment, He was again interrupted by the woman with the issue of blood. "Let me just touch You," she said. After *that* interruption, He continued on His way to heal Jairus's daughter, but he was told that she had died because of the delays. In his mercy, he raises her back up.

Jesus is often thronged with requests: "Raise my son back to life," "Cast the demon out of him," "Open my eyes," "Give me back my legs." Remember that these are not the cries of individuals who had made an appointment! These people came from seemingly nowhere with their issues and inconveniently interrupted Christ as He made His way toward His own cross.

There is a unique principle intertwined in this. In life, you will encounter countless individuals with a cross that develops you as you bear your own cross. As unspiritual as it might sound, there are times when Christians often have the audacity to reply to the Holy Spirit when tapped to take ministerial action or to address a need, "You want me to do *what*?" "When?" "How?" "Surely that was meant for someone else." Many resist the conviction and leading of God's Holy Spirit. Let me make an important warning to those who do. How you respond to the Holy Spirit of God will determine your future.

The Church at Ephesus: A Case in Point

The church at Ephesus had a small beginning; Paul found the church as a congregation of only twelve believers. They had been misinformed about the presence of the Holy Ghost, and seemed to lack a consciousness of the Spirit in the life of the believer. So Paul began his mission there by laying that foundation properly. After about three months of preaching and teaching truth, the Jews hardened their hearts and refused to hear the Gospel. They began to murmur against the message. This, by the way, is a relatable tale for all pastors and church leaders who struggle with whether or not they are effective in their ministry. We judge our influence by how the people we serve live and respond to life issues. Hear me well, my fellow pastors, and be at peace with your ministry assignment: we will always have some parishioners who will not hear the truth. Their responses can range from mild criticism to total unbelief. As Paul found out, people's refusal to hear truth can cause a hardness of heart. A willingness to hear the truth that would have set them free and changed the trajectory of their future.

People respond negatively to truth because it convicts us. Suddenly, the wrongness of our ways is exposed by the brightest of light. And so, it is very important how we respond to the dealings of the Holy Spirit of God as our lives are intersected with ministry opportunities. Let's take a look at a few key areas where the "inconvenience" of Christianity often crops up.

The Inconvenience of Helping the Wounded—God, I'm Too Busy

We can learn some important life principles from the parable Jesus shared in the Book of Luke about a man who fell among thieves. Although it is popularly known as the Parable of the Good Samaritan, and people think it's just about helping others, it is actually a story that deals with two types of relationships: man's relationship with his ways versus God's ways, and man's responses to mankind. Let's deal with the obvious conclusions first, and then move to the more subtle meanings here.

> "A man was going down from Jerusalem to Jericho, when he was attacked by robbers. They stripped him of his clothes, beat him and went away, leaving him half dead. A priest happened to be going down the same road, and when he saw the man, he passed by on the other side. So too, a Levite, when he came to the place and saw him, passed by on the other side. But a Samaritan, as he traveled, came where the man was; and when he saw him, he took pity on him. He went to him and bandaged his wounds, pouring on oil and wine. Then he put the man on his own donkey, brought him to an inn and took care of him. The next day he took out two denarii and gave them to the innkeeper. 'Look after him,' he said, 'and when I return, I will reimburse you for any extra expense you may have.' Which of these three do you think was a neighbor to the man who fell into the hands of robbers?" The expert in the law replied, "The one who had mercy on him." Jesus told him, "Go and do likewise."
>
> (Luke 10:25-37 NIV)

Who Is My Neighbor? My Friends?

This is a question that still confuses many people. Before sharing the parable of the Good Samaritan, Jesus was posed with a question by a lawyer. In this case, the lawyer would have been an expert in the Mosaic Law. The lawyer's question was, "Teacher, what must I do to inherit eternal life?" (Luke 10:25 NIV) Jesus asked him, "What is written in the Law? How do you read it?" (10:26) In response, the lawyer quotes this section of the law: "'Love the Lord your God with all your heart and with all your soul and with all your strength and with all your mind'; and 'Love your neighbor as yourself'" (Luke 10:27 NIV).

Although Jesus could have used this as an opportunity to discuss salvation principles, He chose to focus on our relationship with our fellow humans, our *neighbors*. One of the reasons we know Jesus thought it was wrong to interpret "neighbor" merely as "friend" or "brother" or "comrade" is that in Luke 10:29, when he was asked, "Who is my neighbor?" He answered by telling the parable of the Good Samaritan. In that parable, the man who showed mercy was a Samaritan and the wounded man to whom he showed mercy was a Jew. And the Jews and Samaritans were anything but friends and brothers. They had nothing to do with each other. There were religious and racial animosities between them. This would have intensified the level of inconvenience for the Samaritan, when you review the parable. However, the Samaritan overcame those possible excuses for ignoring him to show mercy. He exhibited God's goodness and answers the question for us all: Who is our neighbor?

The other scenario I want to address is about the first two men who see the beaten Jewish man—the Levite and the priest, both of whom were also Jewish. They didn't have the excuse of religious and racial animosities for reasons not to stop. This leads me to believe that their response to this man's dire need was just an inconvenience of position or title. Allow me to explain. Jesus was calling attention to the two different "levels" of Levites. The Levite (without the authority) knew he shouldn't come in contact with what could possibly have been a dead body since he would, according to the Law of Moses, then become unclean. The priest, however, who was holy, was "particularly charged to avoid uncleanness." Jesus may have been saying that it doesn't matter what "levels" of status they held, either of them should have stopped to show some compassion. Jesus was introducing a new law, a new covenant, and a new kingdom!

What Seems Right, But Ineffective

I preached a message once entitled "The Ineffective Right Way of Doing Nothing." I dealt with this parable from the perspective of the Levitical priesthood. In short, including their mandate to avoid doing anything unclean, I posed the additional possibility of the fact that perhaps the priest in the parable of the Good Samaritan had been on his way to the temple in Jerusalem to perform their duties. Perhaps he intended to pray for the wounded Jewish man once he arrived. But the fact still remains that the man was still in the ditch, still wounded, and possibly dying. Prayer, albeit a good thing to do in general, was an ineffective "right" way of doing nothing! Today, we are still praying that others deal with the responsibilities that we consider to be inconvenient—despite the fact that God has shown us with this parable to personally attend to them.

Ask yourself, "Is it right to do a right thing in a wrong way, and a wrong thing in a right way?" It has been said that the road to hell is paved with good intentions. In fact, Solomon says: "There is a way that seems right to a man, but its end is the way of death" (Proverbs 14:12 ESV). If we look closer at what Solomon is saying, what we will discover is that man, in his 2ignorance and presumptuousness, has thought that whatever he decides to do . . . will do. This is what happens to our sense of sin when God's standards seem no longer to be valid. Our Christian walk starts to move sideways to avoid accountability, then backward away from responsibility, and finally over a twisting detour toward the vulnerability of self-righteousness.

The Inconvenience of Loving Your Enemies—Really, God? You Must Be Joking

So now the plot thickens. Jesus doesn't just say, "I have two commands: one that you love your neighbor and one that you love your enemy." He says, "I have one command: love your neighbor and I mean, even if he is an enemy" (Luke 6:27-36). What? God, this is so not cool! It is absolutely absurd and unreasonable for you to ask me to love someone who clearly doesn't have my best interests at heart. Have you ever felt this way?

I remember saying this during a counseling session to a believer who was dealing with some serious anger issues. "Love my *enemy*?" he said in disbelief when I suggested it. The conversation continued after a somewhat cynical admission on his part. He said, "Sometimes I can't even stand some family members, members of the church, or even coworkers who can be so . . . Well, you know what I mean . . . you know how certain people can be, right?" I replied that God doesn't ask His followers about their opinion concerning whether it was an appealing prospect, He simply demands in the New Testament that we not only tolerate our enemy, quit whining about our enemy, refrain from getting back at our enemy, but also love him or her. As I continued my counseling session and assessed his body language, I began to realize that that there is no teaching in all of scripture more offensive to Christians as what I'll call the command of "enemy-love."

Whereas the Bible says that love is patient and kind, that love is not self-seeking and all that other inconvenient stuff, for many, enemy-love ends up looking inconveniently different than other kinds of love. Instead of "love is patient, love is kind, love is not self-seeking, love never fails," it becomes "love is patient, love is kind, but love chews them up and spits them out if they cross the line with me." Many Christians sadly find it easy to continue to explain away this very clear teaching of Christ in order to cling to their right to bear verbal and emotional weapons to assault, kill, and destroy their enemy.

Who Is My Enemy?

But what did Christ mean by "enemy"? What kind of enmity did He have in mind that qualifies? From the context, we can see an enemy can be a person who commits a wide range of offenses, from very severe opposition to minor snubbing. There are two kinds of love. Both involve the same general feeling, or spring from the same fountain of goodwill toward all humanity. The first is that feeling in which total acceptance is extended in spite of who we are, because of who we are becoming, commonly called the "love of complacency." The second is that feeling in which we wish another person well, though we cannot approve of his or her conduct. This is the "love of benevolence." The latter kind is what we are to bear toward our enemies.

Another way to define an "enemy" is as someone who repeatedly goes against your desires. They may not call themselves your enemies. *You* may not call them enemies. But they resist your will. They are contrary and antagonistic. In this sense, the enemy might be a rebellious church member. He might be an uncaring, stubborn, ill-tempered coworker. He might be a cantankerous neighbor who complains about everything you do to your yard. Jesus says, "Love them. Love your enemies. Love them."

It is impossible to love the *conduct* of a person who curses and reviles us, who injures our person or property, or who violates all the laws of God; but, though we may hate his conduct, and suffer keenly when we are affected by it, yet we may still wish the *person* well. Although we may be disappointed with his foolishness and idiocy, we may speak kindly of him and to him, we may return good for evil, we may aid him in the time of trial, we may seek to do him good here and to promote his eternal welfare hereafter.

This is what Paul speaks of:

> "Do not repay anyone evil for evil. Be careful to do
> what is right in the eyes of everyone. If it is possible, as
> far as it depends on you, live at peace with everyone.
> Do not take revenge, my dear friends, but leave room
> for God's wrath, for it is written: "It is mine to avenge;
> I will repay," says the Lord. On the contrary:
> 'If your enemy is hungry, feed him;
> if he is thirsty, give him something to drink.
> In doing this, you will heap burning coals on his head.'"
> (Romans 12:17-20 NIV)

This seems to be what Jesus meant by loving our enemies. This is a special law of Christianity, the highest possible test of piety, and probably the most difficult of all Christian duties to be performed.

CHAPTER 11

THE BEST-LAID PLANS

The best-laid plans of
mice and men often go awry.
– Robert Burns, *To a Mouse*

Many are the plans in a person's heart,
but it is the Lord's purpose that prevails.
– Proverbs 19:21 (NIV)

WE ALL HAVE PLANS FOR our lives. It may entail chasing a dream that has not been fulfilled yet. It may be meeting a goal within a certain amount of time. There is nothing wrong with making plans for the future or fulfilling dreams. We just need to be careful about how we set out to achieve our goals. The only way to be fully successful is to journey through life with God.

There are times when we get ourselves into circumstances that were not chosen by God, and suddenly we realize that we have been making our plans without Him. As Christians, we understand that all issues are spiritual issues in one way or another. We are counseled to put God first in all things, but we tend to think that it is inappropriate or unnecessary for us to put Him first sometimes—usually until things don't work out the way we expected them to. Because of our pride in our own perceived knowledge, there are times we don't even consider God to be a vital, living factor in the planning of our lives.

Pride of knowledge is a subtle root problem in much of our planning. We simply think we know everything! Sometimes this pride leads to boasting. James gives us some insight about this:

> "Now listen, you who say, 'Today or tomorrow we will go to this or that city, spend a year there, carry on business and make money.' Why, you do not even know what will happen tomorrow . . . Instead, you ought to say, 'If it is the Lord's will, we will live and do this or that." As it is, you boast in your arrogant schemes'" (James 4:13-14a; 15-16a NIV).

Our proper attitude toward making plans should be to make the wisest plans we can,

| It is amazing how God uses our missteps. |

but also to keep our hands and hearts open to accepting or adapting to any changes God wants to make. We may think about the future and plan our lives as carefully as possible, but God has the final word. He is the one who turns our dreams into reality—or who turns our lives in a sharply different direction. God often has a strategic purpose for upsetting the plans we have made when we have not taken Him into account.

We think we know what's best for our own future, but God says, "For my thoughts are not your thoughts, neither are your ways my ways" (Isaiah 55:8 NIV). The reason why God's plan is far better than ours is that He can see the future. He designed it and controls it—we cannot.

When God created us, He already had a perfect and unique plan in place for our lives. With His Kingdom's purpose in mind, He strategically planned out what we would be doing at certain points of our life and what our purpose would serve on behalf of His Kingdom for this life. Then we are born to fulfill that plan. As we go through life, many factors shape our perception and our desires: our family members, our peers in school, what we see around us, and our own desires. We begin to have independent ideas about how we think our life should unfold. But when we really surrender our life to Christ and start seeking out His will for our lives, many of us find that what we had planned was nowhere near what God designed for us. Then there are some of us who find that what we desired to do *is* what God designed for us—but the timing that He uses is not according to the timing that we planned out.

High School Senior Year, Jacksonville, Florida, 1977

I know firsthand what it's like when God interrupts your plans. In fact, I'm living out an example of that right now. I had my life all planned out—what it would look like post high school. I naively set my sights on the aspirations I dreamed of throughout my youth. I assumed that, because I started serving Him at age twelve through my dad's ministry, that He would open doors and bless my plans. Surely they were great plans, right? I thought that He would grant me the resources to fulfill my dreams. After all, it was Him who my dad preached about in the Psalm of David: "Take delight in the Lord, and he will give you the desires of your heart" (Psalm 37:4 NIV).

So there I was, a senior in high school, lying on my bedroom floor, gazing at the ceiling, and daydreaming about my life after graduation. It was four months away. I saw myself attending Howard University, finishing college with an undergraduate degree in business administration, and going on to pursue an MBA while interning with a major corporation. Why *wouldn't* God want that for me?

I had always seen myself as a corporate executive; one day, I planned to branch out to develop a company of my own. I would be a business owner who abided by Christian values. I wanted to get married after I was well established, perhaps in my late thirties, and have the ideal 2.5 children the Gallup polls indicated was the size of the average family. I wanted to plant roots somewhere, buy a home, raise my family, and watch my own kids grow up and go to college and have my grandchildren. Why *wouldn't* God anoint me and my plans? Surely this would be a great achievement for a Christian African American male in today's America.

Then something happened. It wasn't what I desired, but I know now that it was divine. It wasn't what I had planned, but it was His plan, and as He designed it to be. One month before my first semester ended at Howard, I experienced circumstances that began to affect my plans. The kind of situations that make you dive headfirst into *heart-thinking*. It is amazing how God uses our missteps in a single season of our life to guide us toward a path that will lead us to His ultimate will. I didn't know it then, but God was leading me to pursue a vocation in the ministry. He asked me to transfer the same passion I had directed to my academic training for a profession in business toward theological and pastoral training.

The funny thing is that attending a Bible college or seminary had never even occurred to me. Don't get me wrong, I loved reading God's Word. I enjoyed studying the history of how His relationship with man evolved. But that was my father's vocation. Not mine. Not once during my entire youth had I considered entering the ministry as a profession. I only wanted to be a good Christian man. I thought the world already had enough ministers and pastors. Perhaps even too many! Needless to say, I didn't act on God's urging immediately. I continued to work through the conflicts I was experiencing the best way I knew how: under the guise of simply delaying what I was feeling at the time. I was actually avoiding God's will. Yes, like the reluctant prophet Jonah (Jonah 1:3 NIV). I was running away from God's plan.

Not surprisingly, my attempt to outmaneuver God's strategy didn't work out quite like I had hoped. Everything I envisioned in 1977, at the age of eighteen, was just not working out. It was as if I was living in an alternate reality. I was married at twenty-one (not in my late thirties),

> One of the reasons God keeps the intricate details of the journey to Himself is because He values when we try to open up channels of communication with Him.

and by twenty-five I was a father of three lovely kids. After a little over four years of struggling—still stubbornly attempting to merge my own plans with God's plan—and experiencing one discouraging incident after another, one closed door after another, I was forced to sit still and open up my spiritual ears to hear God. This could be translated as the posture you find yourself in when you have tried everything and everyone else but God. This is the place where you find yourself at when all human efforts have failed.

For the first time, I was vulnerable enough to hear God. That could be considered "submission."

Even then, I had doubts lurking in my heart. Did God still want me? Would His calling on my life still be valid? Had I rejected God by trying to avoid His plan for my life?

I didn't feel worthy of any possible future He had designed on my behalf—that would be considered "humility."

Submission and humility. These were the spiritual hearing aids necessary for me to finally communicate with God.

After a season of pondering the questions I had, the idea of a ministry, and actually accepting it, affirmation came from those closest to me. Coincidentally, I found out they had been praying for the same thing! In 1980, I entered the Ministerial Internship Program of the religious denomination I had been involved with since birth. By 1982, I had completed the MIP program and had enrolled in Lee College (now known as Lee University). I packed up my young family, all my meager belongings, and made the journey to Cleveland, Tennessee, to prepare for God's plan in my life.

Over the next thirty-eight years, the divine plans of God deliberately and methodically merged with my own. During this time, I've taken advanced degrees in theology and psychology. I have traveled nationally and internationally preaching, teaching, and lecturing. He inspired me to publish several books. In 2014, I returned to the pastorate. Today I am the senior pastor of an amazing, thriving church in Fort Lauderdale, Florida, and a senior vice president of Logos University in Jacksonville, Florida. We span the globe training and educating individuals for ministry and leadership.

I've had so many life experiences packed into those three decades—some good, and some not so good—that it would be impossible to share them all in one book. I shared quite a few of my defining moments of faith in my previous book, *The God of How*. And I will tell you, while I doubted at times if I made the best choices along the way, God was faithful to *me*. He continued to use His Word as well as the influence of various individuals and circumstances to confirm each and every decision I needed to make according to His will. Little did I know at that time what an unbelievable developmental journey God had designed for me. I can say this now in hindsight, and I do so quite often from my pulpit, that I could never have written a life story with so many strategic twists and turns as my own. Miraculously, they all harmoniously intertwined with His destiny for my life. The shocking and most exciting thing about this story is that it's still unfolding—even today!

God certainly has a way of meeting us right where we are and sometimes of interrupting our plans, dreams, goals, and ideas. The plans and promises God make can be very interesting. God often shows the destination but not the journey, keeping the intricate details of what will befall us on the path along the way to Himself. God's plan is always perfect, maybe not to us, but certainly to Him. In our eyes, the perfect plan is always smooth sailing. But to the wise and all-knowing God, the perfect plan involves churning up enough rough waters along your route to help you build your character and faith. In this way, you are prepared and equipped to receive His promised plan as it unfolds along life's unpredictable journey.

Deciding to Follow God's Plan and Knowing Where to Go Are Two Very Different Things

God keeps the intricate details of our spiritual journey to Himself because He values communication. Especially with those whom He has invested so much of Himself into. If God is in the business of communicating with His people, and His voice has certain distinguishable characteristics, why do we still struggle to hear Him?

Say you are asking God for direction and still you find that your dream-list of your heart's desires is growing longer and longer, and the questions are getting more intense and uncomfortably life-changing. Shouldn't God's answers and plan for our lives be increasingly clearer as well?

To be honest, it can be difficult to hear God's voice at times, and to know which road to take. You pray to God and ask for help, but there are often no prophetic dreams, visions, or strong feelings leading you one way or another. It can seem like God isn't answering you at all. Don't lose heart. God's timing is always perfect—even in His communications to us. Usually, God is waiting for *us* to be sincere before He speaks. As I said earlier, submission and humility are the hearing aids necessary for communication with God.

God makes an amazing promise in the book of Jeremiah:

> "For I know the plans I have for you," declares the Lord, "plans to prosper you and not to harm you, plans to give you hope and a future. Then you will call on me and come and pray to me, and I will listen to you. You will seek me and find me **when you seek me with all your heart.**"
>
> (Jeremiah 29:11-13 NIV)

Submission and humility are the attributes of a sincere heart. This is the prerequisite for God to speak and for you to hear. Wouldn't it be great to always know what God wants you to do in a given situation and be 100 percent sure you are planning and doing the right thing? There is a well-known anonymous quote which says that, "Life's greatest discovery is to know the will of God and life's greatest satisfaction is to do the will of God." When you know His will for your life and do His will, your life will be filled with a purpose that brings unbelievable joy, peace, and satisfaction.

Our difficulty in hearing God's voice is matched by another problem we have—following God's plan once we *are* able to hear Him. This problem stems from an apparent issue with authority. At times, it is not so apparent, and can even lead to a place of living in denial. The writings of C. S. Lewis and Sigmund Freud help us understand one difficulty we often have in seeing the signposts that points all mankind to God: namely, our tendency to distort our image of God. One of Freud's theories proves the unconscious process of transference. This is the tendency to displace feelings from authority figures in our childhood onto those in the present, thus distorting and causing conflict with present authority.

If his theory holds true, we must be careful that our concept of God—whether the God we reject as unbelievers or that we worship as believers—is firmly based on the Creator revealed in history and not on our neurotic distortion of Him.[1] It is important how we view God, because that will determine how we view our life, God's plan for it, and how we respond to Him.

YOU HAVE A CHOICE

You can say "no" to the plan God suggests and go your own way. But that choice has certain consequences. If you reject God's will, however, you will miss the best things God has planned for you. The best-laid plans are not your own, they are God's. Attempting to squeeze your plans into God's life for you is like living life with your left shoe on your right foot—it's just not a good fit and will surely cause you to stumble. At most, your life will be a pale shadow of what it was meant to be. It won't be the wonderful life God had planned for you.

The fact is, God made you. He fashioned you, loves you, and knows what is best for you. He wants your life to be filled with the *best* things life has to offer. We're not talking about material wealth, but rather the fulfillment of completing God's real purpose and plans for your life. In eternity, that is what will matter. That is why it simply makes good sense to align your life with God and do His will.

Do you really want a life outside the will of God? Because you are reading this, you're likely searching for ways to discover God's best plans for you. You've come to the right place, because He *does* want you to know His best. He has the plan for your life, and you have a choice to make.

CHAPTER 12

MISTAKEN IDENTITY

He who belongs to God hears what God says.
— John 8:47 (NIV)

The Theology of Identity—Its Beginning in Genesis

YOUR PERSONAL IDENTITY IS TIED to the posture of your personal spirit. Ever get the feeling that nobody really knows the real you? It may be a question of whether or not you know yourself. The central narrative development of Genesis 1:26 stresses that our true identity has its conception at the point of creation. The language in that passage is profound, and it raises the significant point that we are made in the image of God. This is an important distinction—one that separates mankind from all other creatures, not between the subcategories of male and female.

It is only regarding the creation of mankind that God says, "Let us make man in our own image," and God only directly breathed into man's nostrils the breath of life (Genesis 1:26, 2:7 NIV). Everything in the text of Genesis 1 and 2 describes the intimate actions God took in creating mankind (both the first man and the first woman) compared to the general approach He took to creating everything else.

The issue with the first humans was that they were tempted into exploring an identity apart from God. It was His Spirit that connected us to His identity. Man desired to be superior to God, just as Satan had prior to his eviction from Heaven. And man has since endeavored to this sense of superiority, which has become our plight in a world of mistaken identities. This mindset is evident in the writings of Friedrich Nietzsche. In his book *Beyond Good and Evil*, as translated by R. J. Hollingdale, Nietzsche contends that "every superior human being will instinctively aspire after a secret citadel where he is set free from the crowd, the many, the majority, where, as its exception, he may forget the rule of 'man.'" [1]

God's purpose in giving us our identity was not so that we would focus on trying to achieve a sense of superiority. *Our* identity is for the sake of making known *God's* identity. You are God's masterpiece. (Ephesians 2:10 NLT). A masterpiece is defined as "a person's greatest work of art," or a "consummate example of skill or excellence." Now, when God's Word describes you as His masterpiece, it is referring to His assessment of you, not what you think, nor what others think. Over the course of our lives, each person's identity is formed and shaped through individual experiences, relationships, culture, media, and the world around us. We are constantly seeking to define who we are in any way that we can. God's assessment of who we are is the only one that matters.

The Image of God and Our Identity Is Not Our Body

Humanity is created in the image of God—this fact carries numerous implications for the identity of man, the nature of his interpersonal relationships, the lens through which he views existence, and the foundation and mission of the church.

The human body is something that makes the human creaturely. It is the unique creation of mankind in the image of God that distinguishes us from all other creatures. As was stated previously, out of all God's creation, He chose only to directly breathe into *man's* nostrils the breath of life. The breath of God that surged through a body made from the dust became the image of God. Our identity is divinely and uniquely interwoven in God's image.

Individuals today tend to define themselves by their body image, by what they do and not who they are, by virtue of their associations rather than by virtue of their Godly origin. Tracing the anthropology of man shows his identity is rooted in being created in the image of God.

Throughout church history, there has been much debate about the effect of sin on the image of God in man. Even so, there are three unifying truths. First, the Bible teaches that even after sin, mankind is still created in God's image (Genesis 9:6; James 3:8-9). Second, sin has devastatingly affected the image of God in man (Romans 3:23; Isaiah 59:1-4). Third, we lost our identity!

In Search of Lost Identity

The temptation of Adam and Eve revolves around their identity as God's offspring. When the serpent tempted Eve in Genesis 3:1-5, he not only told her lies, he also called God a liar.

God said not to eat of the fruit of one particular tree in the garden. According to Genesis 2:17, they were told not to eat from that tree for their own protection: if they did, they would "certainly die." Nothing in the narrative to this point, however, had given Adam and Eve any reason to question God's motives for this prohibition. They simply obeyed. The serpent undermines God's word to Adam and Eve concerning the tree of knowledge of good and evil with three counterclaims, each of which tempts them to seek to establish their own autonomy and an identity independent of God:

1. You will not die; instead,
2. Your eyes will be opened; and
3. You will be like God.

The serpent's lies were designed to undermine Adam and Eve's confidence in God and to tempt them to find an identity independent of Him. In succumbing to the serpent's lies, they turned from God and lost their association *and* identity. From that time until now, mankind has struggled with and been in search of an identity apart from God.

What's behind this struggle over identity? It comes down to worldview. Because we are made in the image of God, God is the fixed reference point on which our design, purpose, and value are established. If we want to know who we are, we must start by looking up (at Him), not around (at others) or within (at ourselves).

> You have a God-identity through Christ that the world will always refuse to connect you with.

The problem is, we primarily associate the search for identity with the affirmation of those around us. The struggle and search for identity begins during our early teenage years. Young people begin the path of "finding themselves," questioning the messages they receive from authority figures, pushing boundaries, etc. The search for identity continues well beyond adolescence for many, and may be a lifelong process for others.

Mistaken Identity

I entered my office one morning, turned the lights on, and began my normal routine to start my day. I sat my briefcase down and turned on my espresso machine. After preparing my very much needed cup of espresso, I logged on to my computer and into my counseling software to review my files for the day ahead.

I tried to open a particular church member's file, but I couldn't get her name to appear in the search bar. I tried once again, and then again. Her name *wouldn't* appear. I was perplexed. This had never happened before. Glancing at the top of the search window, I realized I actually wasn't logged into the counseling software I use for church members. The day before I had forgotten to sign off, and my computer had been on sleep mode throughout the night. When I turned on my computer, it still had the last user account and file open from the day before, which was a ministry mentorship program. I use a separate account for counseling to keep counseling documents and assignments organized and confidential. Because I have two login identities for the two separate accounts, I couldn't get where I wanted to go because I had a case of mistaken identity.

With a quick click of the mouse, I switched accounts and accessed the right account and program. By using the right identity, I was free to access my counseling clients, review my notes for our meetings later that day, leave comments with ease, and navigate through all the files I needed—moving from folder to folder and file to file.

Sometimes in life we encounter the same issue, on a different scale. A mistaken identity can keep us from living out God's best plan for our lives. This may happen when a voice from our past or our own negative self-image causes us to forget our identity in Christ. We log in to our day and encounter wrong thinking that's not in sync with who we are. Those wrong thoughts lead us to doubt God's promise of a life filled with security, significance, and purpose. Although *who we are* should be deeply rooted in who God has declared and proclaimed that we are in Him, we experience seasons in our life that leave us questioning our value as a person.

Instead of the truth of our identity, we hear the voices of social, cultural, and educational discrimination and stereotyping saying: *You can't do this or that*, and *You aren't good enough.* We also hear voices from a little closer to home: from family, friends, and enemies who might have once been friends telling you: *You'll never change. Why can't you be more like your sister or brother? If only you were more X instead of so Y.*

We must all recognize that the world around us is really attempting to shape not only our identities, but also our belief system, our desires, our habits, and every aspect of life that defines us in this world. The internet and social media are at the forefront of this dilemma. The many voices in this modern world must not be allowed to dictate who you are and what you are capable of. You have a God-identity through Christ that the world will always refuse to connect you with. There is an amazing Spirit within you that can release unlimited power and creative imagination—something that this world will never understand. And what people don't understand they usually reject and attempt to disqualify.

Sometimes these people are not only around you, but in your head. They are the voices that taunt you whenever you set a goal. That criticize you when life gets difficult. They beat you down when you struggle to stand up against their devaluing commentary. You know you should not let the self-doubt bother you, but it is a cunning and subtle beast. Sometimes, you find yourself unable to resist it and it slips past your spiritual barriers. Self-doubt is greedy, and when it is released it will devour your confidence, strip Godly reasoning from your mind, and steal joy from your heart and peace from your soul.

In return, it leaves you with only fear, anxiety, and insecurity. When self-doubt screams and discouragement sets in, we need to recognize what's happening, log out of the lies we are tempted to believe, and log in to God's truth. It's the only way to live in our true identity so we can navigate our lives according to God's Word.

Identify and Ease Identity Doubts

Honoré de Balzac, a French novelist and playwright, once said, "When you doubt your power, you give power to your doubt." It is crucial that we recognize when our self-talk or others'-talk takes a turn for the worse. When you hear yourself or others saying, "You can't," or "You don't know," or "What if," a red flag should go up in your spirit. The human perspective on identity is tenuous at best and downright venomous at worst. When we look to outside sources to define who we are, we aren't going to get an accurate picture. When we rely on others to tell us who we are, we are not only in danger of losing touch with our true selves, but we are also in danger of caving in to every peer pressure imaginable in order to win outside approval.

So, what should define us? Or rather, *who* should have the final say about who we are? Ultimately, we need to be listening to the one whose view of us is completely accurate, the one who cannot lie, the one who is consistently stable in every way. If you think the answer to these questions is you, you are sadly mistaken. We each can be easily deceived.

At moments like this, it is vital that we remember what the

apostle John tells us: "He who belongs to God hears what God says" (John 8:47 NIV). We need to be more attentive to His Word rather than to self-talk. Let what God says about you take root in your mind and allow it to eradicate any untrue, destructive thought patterns. Replacing the negative chatter with assuring scriptures will gently but firmly remind us of our true identity—we are children of God.

Yes, there will always be people who are convinced that the person they see in the mirror every morning is real, or who will buy into the superimposed image others have engraved onto us. And because they are convinced of this identity, they are quick to shoot down any idea of a different view of themselves—or even a different life for themselves. But remember, if we "belong to God," we will hear what He says. And as we log in to His truths daily, no longer will we mistake our identity or our possibilities. We will know the confident reality of who we are in Christ.

Trust God, Know Yourself, and Love Yourself

Our quest to become the best version of ourselves begins with trusting God and loving yourself—your God-self. Many individuals spend more time being their own worst enemy instead of being their own best friend. Even Christ tells us the importance of loving yourself—not in an arrogant prideful way, of course. Here is what He says:

> "Jesus said: The first in importance is, 'Listen, Israel: The Lord your God is one; so, love the Lord God with all your passion and prayer and intelligence and energy.' **And here is the second: 'Love others as well as you love yourself.'** There is no other commandment that ranks with these."
>
> (Mark 12:30-31 MSG)

In essence, your ability to love others is rooted in your ability to love yourself. That is, having a sober appreciation of who you are and the value God has placed on your life. With this in mind, we must all learn to treat ourselves better. After all, you have the rest of your life to spend with yourself. So get to know the true you. I believe one of the most tragic things to experience in life is to not know who you are living with, in your own body. I always tell couples who come to me for premarital counseling that if you don't know who you are, then you don't know who you are giving to someone else. You must first make a covenant with God, then you can make one with someone else. That pertains to both individuals—unless strangers want to marry.

Give Yourself Permission to Reimagine Yourself in God

Mistaken identity and self-doubt never just disappear. Over time, you simply get better at dealing with them. They will greet you every time you fall out of your comfort zone and whenever you strive to do something amazing with your life. You must get to a place where this occurrence is not something you fear or resent. Your mistaken identity is just an illusion, and your doubts are only thoughts, not your future. You already have within you the best image of all, since God created you in His image. Focus on discovering more about what God's image looks like in you, and how you can express it more in your life.

You have to give yourself permission to see a different "you." Give yourself permission to explore life by experiencing God's guided tour of this world through His will and His purpose.

Eradicate the Roadblocks

Identify the roadblocks that affect you most and prevent you from seeing yourself as God sees you. This will involve looking beyond cultural images to the image of God in you. Don't settle for simply taking on a particular image that appeals to you. In our modern society, it is so easy to fall prey to lure of convincing ourselves we need to be popular, sexy, glamorous, tough, afro-centric, euro-centric, suburbanite, inner-city, or something else. Realize that these images are all superficial. Behind their appeal is a God-given longing to be everything God wants you to be. Recognize that the urge you feel to take on certain worldly images is really a desire to grow.

Another roadblock you must break through is your feelings' dominion over your decision-making process. When you don't know who you really are, you become a slave to your feelings, constantly reacting to them and becoming confused when they change. Trusting God rather than your feelings for your sense of identity is sometimes tough, but it is crucial. He will give you a solid foundation that remains the same no matter how changing circumstances affect your feelings. Trusting God will guard your heart and mind in any situation.

The next roadblock to break through involves recognizing that you become like whatever you worship. When you derive your sense of self from secular cultural images and philosophies communicated through the media, you're essentially worshipping them. That image will then come to control you. And when this happens, it turns you into a poor imitation of who you were meant to be. Remember that all humans are created in the image of God, and only in finding our identity in God can we experience life in all its fullness. We can recover the image of God in our lives by finding our ultimate identity. And we do this by reflecting and representing God on earth—as His beloved children.

PART III

UNDERSTANDING GOD AND BOUNDARIES

CHAPTER 13

UNDER PRESSURE

Our Father, when we long for life without trials
and work, without difficulties, remind us that
oaks grow strong in contrary winds and
diamonds are made under pressure.
With stout hearts may we see in every calamity
an opportunity and not give way to the pessimist
that sees in every opportunity a calamity.

– Peter Marshall

PETER MARSHALL WAS A SCOTS-AMERICAN preacher, pastor of the New York Avenue Presbyterian Church in Washington, DC, and twice-appointed chaplain of the United States Senate. His prayer summarizes the focus of this chapter so well. The average person today faces a myriad of different pressures. Attempting to navigate through the challenges in life without some kind of strategic controls or manageable structure can impact our physical, emotional, and psychological well-being.

We must begin with the importance of the basic principle of *understanding*. Understandings flow out of insights. Understandings are also dependent on insights. Understandings are the applications of insights to daily life. In Proverbs, the Bible places great emphases on the value of understanding:

"Get wisdom, get understanding; do not forget my
words or turn away from them.
Do not forsake wisdom, and she will protect you; love
her, and she will watch over you. The beginning of
wisdom is this: Get wisdom. Though it cost all you
have, get understanding."

(Proverbs 4:5-7 NIV)

Psychology teaches that in the mental life it should come as no
surprise to realize that, out of the basic consciousness God has
enacted on our behalf in Christ, believers' ability to "understand" the
triumphs and tragedies of life through the eyes of faith. Understandings
are like glasses that Christians put on to apply their faith to the way
they interpret the events of their lives—both events that happen to
them and events they cause. [1]

The key to understanding pressure is understanding the
relationship it has with faith. Helping parishioners deal with stress
is a basic goal of all ministers
and pastors. I am not aware
of any pastor who does *not*
desire that faith become

> Stress will always appear first in
> the weakest areas of your life.

personal in some way to those whom they minister to at some point
in their life, so that they can use it to help them through life's most
difficult moments. Faith is merely theory in the life of the believer,
however, until the influence of pressure places a demand on your
belief system to act *or not*. Only then is faith forced to become a
conscious insight and a reality, even for those who grew up never
identifying themselves as anything other than a Christian.

There are pressures of society, the effects of government on our
economy, employment issues, and the predicament of unpredictable
stress and tension in twenty-first-century relationships. They become
so complex that faith and strategic boundaries are necessary to
appropriately manage them. Would you be surprised if I told you that
the Bible gives us examples of Jesus setting personal boundaries and
practicing self-care? Life is a blank canvas of complicated scenarios

waiting to happen. Pressures hover. We must use the hands of *choice* to fill in our canvas with colorful experiences. Most of them range from cool strokes of sky blue, which might represent mild testing, to intense, fire-red splashes of chaos and mayhem. Nevertheless, they are part and parcel of everything we do. The bottom line is that they are unavoidable.

As a senior pastor, pressure comes at me from many different directions. I have to worry about things that no one else in the church does. If something goes wrong, I get the call or an email. If something bad happens, I get blamed. That's part of the job, but this pressure, just like whatever pressure you might feel in your job, causes stress. Sometimes we express that we're stressed in relationships, in mounting frustration, or in outbursts of exasperation. For me, stress tends to play havoc with my health. Wherever I am the weakest, the stress appears.

Stress will always appear first in the weakest areas of your life. If your relationships are weak, then the pressures of life will begin to build stress there first. That is the nature of this emotional monster. If you have a quick temper, then pressure will intensely compress that temper nerve and you are much more apt to snap or get angry.

The pressures of ministry and the trials that encompass God's plan for me are something I gladly accept, however. Ministry is my purpose and my cause. It is my life. Because I am aware of God's purpose for my life and I absolutely trust Him with everything in my life, the pressures of the ministry and life are not loathsome or revolting to me. The stress, however, can grind me into dust, if I let it. I need effective boundaries to manage and reduce much of the stress that the pressure produces in my life. And I must strengthen those areas in my life that are the weakest. If I don't do that, the stress can become overwhelming.

The same is true for you. You need to put a mechanism in place to deal with the pressures of life. Then you need means, methods, and boundaries for reducing the stress that the pressure produces. Remember, the stress always appears first in your most vulnerable and weakest areas.

Why Is It Important to Set Boundaries?

Unless there are boundaries, we overdo it in ministering to others, get worn out in relationships, and even burnout on life! Jesus had far more stress, far more pressure, and far more responsibility than any of us, and yet he remained relaxed, joyful, and generous with people. He models for us how to live by accepting God's rhythms of grace and allowing them to mediate our stress—even under extreme pressure.

Personal boundaries are a part of how God further defines your identity in Him. They're like the property lines around a home. They alert us, as well as others, where you start and end. This is me. This is what I value. This is what I am good at. This is what I believe in. This is what I need the most. This is what I feel—what is for me and what is not for me.

To know yourself and feel secure, and know that you are loved, is essential to all of your relationships and essential to properly managing life's issues. The better your boundaries of self-awareness and self-definition in God are, the greater your capacity to stand under pressure. Good boundaries also help you to care for others, because they give you a stable foundation to operate from, and they keep you from feeling distracted or depleted by personal insecurities or blind spots. In the previous chapter, I quoted Christ advocating the second-most-valuable commandment: *love your neighbor as you love yourself.* That's why it's not "selfish" or unloving to have boundaries and "take care of yourself."

Is Pressure Always Bad?

Stress and pressure keep us working. We are driven by them. Sometimes, we suppress them. We deny that they exist other times, or even try to escape them. We take vitamins to help our bodies deal with them. We feel them in our chest. Our stomach stirs and aches. Our heart palpitates, and our palms get sweaty. And all of us are gripped by stress at some points.

The questions for all of us are: How do we live with stress? Is pressure always bad? Here is really where God's reasoning seems unreasonable to man's logic. James connects the dots of God's plan behind life's pressures and their purposes in our life. Pay close attention. Don't miss it:

> "Consider it a sheer gift, friends, when tests and challenges come at you from all sides. You know that under pressure, your faith-life is forced into the open and shows its true colors. So, don't try to get out of anything prematurely. Let it do its work so you become mature and well-developed, not deficient in any way."
> (James 1:2-4 MSG)

Seriously, God? Somehow, we are not able to initially understand that, by giving us pressure, God is showing us love. Does he have to do it under intense circumstances? It's like a parent telling a child, "I know it hurts, but I'm chastising you because I love you." I remember hearing that from my parents during my adolescence. Only "chastise" back then was a cute word for a whooping! For this younger generation, who can't quite relate to that word (whooping), it can be defined as one level above spanking. The point is to inflict pain as an incentive not to misbehave or as a "deterrent" (that too was a euphemism in my day). The rod of correction was usually in the form of a belt or your choice of a "switch" from a bush—and you'd better choose wisely, because you certainly didn't want your parent to choose the switch.

I digress. Back to my parents explaining why the "whooping" was for my own good. They said they were doing it because they loved me. I would always say (under my breath of course), "Well, if that's love, just hate me why don't you?" If they could have heard my response, I would have gotten more of their "love!" I laugh at those times now—only because I understand them.

Likewise, God left us a book that was meant to be a guide to achieving a cursory understanding of His ways. He tells us that His ways are ultimately beyond our understanding, but that He has chosen to give us a clue to help us live righteously. He desires that we understand His general reasoning. It doesn't matter how great the pressure is, only where the pressure lies. If we make sure it never comes between us and God, then the greater the pressure, the more it presses us to conform to His set boundaries. Each pressure in life is like a divine gravitational pull, tugging us toward a rationale that will help us come into alignment with His plans for us, drawing us closer to Him and the nature of His love.

Human Nature and Pressure

But sometimes you just want out. Don't you? We often think less stress would be better. Sometimes, that is true. However, many of us also want to avoid even having to deal with the things that are good for us to bear. There *can* be positive side-effects of pressure. It is not pressure, but our response to pressure, that determines pressure's effect on us.

When a crisis arises, the worst mistake you can make is to pretend that nothing is wrong. It can sometimes feel like you're carrying a piano on your back. Although the concept of pressure and stress was originally defined in terms of its physiological mechanism, the human response to stress or any threat of pressure on human nature is complex. It is a psychosocial and spiritual reality of human life. Stress is a term used to include a broader meaning, such as suffering, which is a personal response to painful circumstances and deficiencies.

There are the pressures of want, need, sorrow, pain, persecution, unpopularity, or loneliness. Some suffer for what *they* have done; others suffer because of what people have done *to* them. Many suffer because they are victims of circumstances beyond their control. Pain and suffering are distressing. There can be nights of agony, when God seems so unfair and it seems there is no possible help or answer for your situation. As I said earlier, we must keep in mind that it is not pressure, but our response to pressure, that determines pressure's effect on us.

The solution is to condition our attitudes so that we learn to triumph in and through suffering. When Paul looked for relief from his "thorn in the flesh" (2 Corinthians 12:7 NKJV), God did not take it away (although there may be times that He does), but He told him that "My grace is sufficient for you, for my strength is made perfect in weakness" (2 Corinthians 12:9 NKJV).

There is nowhere in the Bible that teaches that just because you are a Christian you are exempt from the trials and tribulations that come upon any and all of the

> Our attitude to suffering should glorify God. This is important, because people are going to watch us as Christians.

people of the world. However, Scripture does teach that the Christian can face tribulation, crisis, calamity, and personal suffering with a supernatural power that is not available to the person outside of relationship with Christ.

Those of us who are in relationship with Christ should believe wholeheartedly in the sovereignty of God during difficult trials. Yet, sometimes, we tend to elevate the attribute of God's sovereignty over all His other attributes. We do this because we're hurting badly, and we need someone to blame. We may even say to ourselves, "I know He can change things, He's just choosing not to. Why?"

Yes, He *could* change things, though he doesn't always choose to. This then, presses us into accepting and trusting in the goodness of God in order to trust in God's sovereign will. Otherwise, we sinfully blame Him for what we perceive as problems. We may not realize we blame God like this. Perhaps we respond to our circumstances by affirming God's sovereignty with our lips, even when we don't actually believe in His goodness in our hearts. When we do this, we separate two characteristics of God—His sovereignty and His goodness. As a result, we paint an inaccurate picture of God's true nature.

Look at the pressure Job was under to maintain his faith in the goodness of God. Job did plenty of questioning: Has God forgotten me? Does He hate me? Why does He seem to hide Himself from me? These questions reflected what his human nature was attempting to convince his mind to accept—a very different picture of the God he worshipped prior to his suffering.

Here is the "unreasonable" reasoning we find in Job's story: Job was blameless and upright. He was a man of such integrity that God wanted to show him off. We would all agree then that if anyone deserved to be blessed by God, Job would qualify as the perfect candidate. No, he didn't deserve what was happening to him. But the fact is that we do bring some suffering upon ourselves; that's not to say all suffering is our fault. The innocent suffers too. In His justice, God knows and understands that this will seem unjust to us.

Why God Allows Pressure to Affect Us

The reality of why God allows pressure and suffering to bother the innocent as well as the guilty is a paradoxical truth that paralyzes the faith of many. The Apostle Paul knew this was a complicated concept. He begged God to take away the thorn in his flesh, but Christ said, "My grace is sufficient for you, for my power is made perfect in weakness" (2 Cor. 12:9 NIV). Don't miss the critical point here. It wasn't that Paul rose above his pain, the point is that he was still weak, but Christ gave him the strength to stand firm and press on through and beyond his pain. Paul was no triumphant victor over suffering, he was a man who feared and trembled, who was whipped, stoned, and hungry. He was imprisoned and deserted by his friends (see: 1 Cor. 2:3; 2 Cor. 11:23-29; 2 Tim. 4:16).

Our attitude during times of suffering should glorify God. People are going to watch us as Christians. They will ask, "How is it that Christ is so in control of his or her life that he or she was able to withstand such attacks?" How? Well, the *how* is an easy answer—His grace is sufficient to get us through any situation. It is the *why* that baffles us. When you've passed through your own fiery trials, you discover God to be true to what he says. Paul said of this of his time in Asia:

> "We were under great pressure, far beyond our ability to endure, so that we despaired of life itself. Indeed, we felt we had received the sentence of death. **But this happened that we might not rely on ourselves but on God**, who raises the dead."

> (2 Cor 1:8-9 NIV)

Perhaps the point is still elusive. What good can be had from God allowing us to feel pressure and pain? Where is the joy in suffering? It comes from using it to help us discover more of God. It comes from developing more dependence on God (2 Corinthians 1:9). It comes from lessening our desire to sin (2 Corinthians 12:7), deepening our faith, and increasing our capacity for everlasting, unshakeable joy. All these things can only come to us through the refining process of pain and suffering.

As believers, we will be given firsthand experience, like Paul, of both His sustaining grace and His purposeful design. Upon reflection, you will see that He has upheld you through the pressures and pain of life. He has reshaped you more into his image. But here's the next benefit of suffering: What you are experiencing through God, you can *give away* in increasing measure to others. Believe it or not, those who suffer want to be ministered to by people who have suffered. They are suspicious of people who appear to live lives of ease. You are learning both the tenderness and the clarity necessary to help sanctify another person's deepest distress and pain.

When we try to help others by engaging with their pain, encourage them to have the patience to let God speak to the situation. It is a hard, but necessary, experience for members of our faith. Joy in Christ will ultimately enable us to persevere and heal with hope and confidence. He knows what we need better than we do. Like a master physician with a painful prescription, his ultimate goal is not to harm us, but a painful cure may be the only way for us to achieve our greatest good. We need to be careful not to wallow in self-pity and bitterness. Our God is a good God. He is sovereign over all things—even what seems bad.

I don't know what role God has for you, but I know He *has* a role. His great passion is expressed in His Great Commission, and He has given it to people under pressure, like you and me. He has made us His ambassadors of reconciliation, and suffering gives us credibility with a hurting world and demonstrates God's sufficiency to meet our needs.

CHAPTER 14

BLURRED LINES (TRUSTING GOD? OR TESTING GOD?)

1. a situation where things are **ambiguous** or **unclear**.
2. Sometimes meaning **"to push the envelope"**
or **test the boundaries of acceptability**.
— Urban Dictionary

WE ARE UNUSUALLY COMFORTABLE WITH ambiguity in our world. People are too comfortable living their lives within what I call a "blurred line reality." You could define this as a perspective drawn from our human nature and its desires. Humans tend to operate primarily in the sense realm, which is influenced by our five senses (*touch, sight, hearing, smell,* and *taste*). These five senses provide us with the ability to experience and respond to carnal reality; however, the fact that we all also have imaginations means that we are also capable of experiencing the far greater and complex realm of illusions.

An illusion is a misleading perception of reality or a belief misconception. The world in which we live, however, is perceived by *interpreting* what we see, hear, and experience through our primary five senses. When these senses are underdeveloped, it's easier to create misleading spiritual illusions. That's where the lines of righteousness start to blur. The fine lines that we tend to use as boundaries between acceptable and unacceptable behavior blur easily with our futile attempts to justify our sins.

I have always found it amazing how, out of the five natural senses God designed when creating mankind, David used only two of them to describe experiencing the sweetness of God's character:

> "Oh, **taste** and **see** that the Lord is good;
> blessed is the one who takes refuge in him."
> (Psalm 34:8 NIV)

David continues by saying:

> "I remain confident of this:
> I will **see** the goodness of the Lord
> in the land of the living."(Psalm 27:13 NIV)

David highlights just two of our five senses, but the authority of a life lived in God is contingent on the fact that our whole body is needed by God. A full surrender and transformation of our five senses from carnality to spirituality is paramount for avoiding the delusions and illusions nurtured in the realm of blurred-line reality. The transformation of our senses is only possible through a relationship with God, which is facilitated by the regenerating power of God's Spirit and the power of His Word.

But most of society today sees God's Word and His plans as too demanding and inconvenient. People settle for the control they have over the world they perceive, and are quite comfortable with the blurry lines in their life. They're comfortable because we live in a "don't judge me," "don't tell me what to do," and "anything goes" kind of world. People *want* the lines to be blurry, because then there is no accountability. People embrace the blurry lines as long as they appear to lean more "their way."

In his book *The Sacrament of Psychology*, Richard Cox makes a comparison between humanistic accountability versus God's view of accountability. He states that, "Accountability in today's church has taken on a psychological definition which is highly humanistic and measures one against oneself. We ask, 'Are you being true to yourself?' That is not the question from church history or from theology. That question is straight out of humanistic psychology. The question of the church has to do with being true to your God, your community, your church, your brothers and sisters, *and yourself*, as well as being true to eternal truth and dimensions of action that require more than your own strength. A tall demand—not a user-friendly suggestion."[1]

Blurring the Lines of Faith

In his commentary on Charles Taylor's book, James K. A. Smith writes, "even as faith endures in our secular age, believing doesn't come easy . . . We don't believe instead of doubting; we believe while doubting."[2] For some, trusting in God can feel next to impossible. It is in our nature to want control of our own lives and to do things our way. When we feel like we have control, we feel like we're operating in a comfort zone. There is that misconception of belief that if we are in control of our lives or a situation, we won't let anything go wrong. And when something does go wrong, we're even less likely to give up what little control we may actually have.

Others blur the lines of faith by using the idea of testing God as a form of trusting Him. God is clear about how He feels on the matter of being tested. The Bible gives us examples of acceptable and unacceptable ways of testing God. However, the ways in which it is acceptable to test God are far more limited than the ways in which it is unacceptable to test Him. Many times, we test God because we doubt Him. A test rooted in unbelief is unacceptable. This is a point I would like to take a closer look at in the second part of our discussion of "blurred lines." Its meaning suggest that this occurs when someone chooses "to push the envelope" or "to test the boundaries of acceptability."

To my knowledge, the only occurrence specifically mentioned in the Bible where God welcomes anyone to test Him regards tithes and offerings is found in the book of Malachi:

"Bring the full tithe into the storehouse, that there may be food in my house. **And thereby put me to the test, says the LORD of hosts,** if I will not open the windows of heaven for you and pour down for you a blessing until there is no more need."

(Malachi 3:10 ESV)

"Test," in this verse, is translated from the Hebrew word *Bachan*. It means "to examine, scrutinize, or prove (as in gold, persons, or the heart)." As putting gold in a fire tests its quality, God invited the Israelites to test Him by giving their tithes and offerings. In return, He proved His faithfulness to them.

However, there is another Hebrew word used for "test" in the Bible, *nacah*, which means "to put to the test, try, or tempt." This word is used in Deuteronomy 6:16, a verse in which God commands the Israelites *not* to test Him. This is the posture people who operate in the blurred line reality take when approaching God—they foolishly test Him under the guise of wanting to see if they can really trust Him. They are pushing the proverbial envelope—testing the boundaries of God's acceptability. If they feel the need to test Him, that means that they do not actually have faith to trust Him at all. In most cases, testing God is unacceptable. This is because it tends to be rooted in our own doubt of God's faithfulness.

The Blurred Lines of Israel Testing God

In Exodus, Chapter 16, we see Israel leaving the Desert of Sin, where God's miraculous provision of manna had commenced. The Israelites went from place to place, as the Lord directed them. It is significant to note that, at this point, the Israelites are totally unaware that God is in no hurry to deliver them into the promised land of Canaan. In Chapter 17, we find them at another place along the way to Canaan, called Massah.

They set up camp in Massah, but soon discovered there was no water there. The Israelites grumbled to Moses. Since Moses had been able to miraculously sweeten the waters at Marah and to produce quail and manna, the people appear to be demanding that he perform another miracle for them. It is as though he must prove he has God's authority to lead them by producing water miraculously. The Israelites should have learned by then to trust God to supply their needs. It is bad enough that the Israelites argued with Moses and demanded that he provide them with water; in effect, they were also challenging God as well:

> "Therefore, the people quarreled with Moses and said, 'Give us water to drink.' And Moses said to them, 'Why do you quarrel with me? Why do you **test the LORD?**' But the people thirsted there for water, and the people grumbled against Moses and said, 'Why did you bring us up out of Egypt, to kill us and our children and our livestock with thirst?'"
>
> (Exodus 17:2-3 ESV)

This story shows us that grumbling and complaining test God. It is the same type of uncertainty as when we question Him about whether or not He is with us. Both of these things count as testing Him, because they reveal our own unbelief and mistrust. They show that we do not trust Him because we think He is not providing for us in the way we think we ought to be provided for, but of course we cannot know the entirety of His plan for us.

The Blurred Lines of Satan's Temptation

The temptation narrative between Jesus and the devil recalls the testing of Israel in the wilderness and provides a model for the blurred-line test all believers are subject to taking. When Jesus was fasting in the wilderness, the gospel of Matthew records that the devil came to tempt

> The integration of Christian faithfulness into our daily life is complex and key to our relationship with God.

Him (Matthew 4:1-11). The devil proposed that Jesus "prove" that God's promises were true by doing several things that would force God to move on His behalf—to turn stones into bread, to jump off the temple, and to reject God for worldly power and prestige.

Of the several suggestions the devil presented, I want to focus on one. It is where the devil wants Jesus to put Himself in harm's way—to throw Himself off the highest point of the temple in the holy city of Jerusalem. The devil's "convincing" argument was similar to the others in that it revolved around taking God's word out of context. He proposed that if Jesus were to put Himself in danger, God would have no choice but to save Him. Jesus refused to fall prey to this trap, and quoting the very clear line about God's righteous and our response to His righteousness from Deuteronomy 6:16 as a rebuff:

> "Away from me, Satan! Jesus declared. For it is written: 'Worship the Lord your God and serve Him only.'"
> (Matthew 4:10 BSB)

Just as Jesus quoted Scripture to ward off the devil, so can we. God is faithful about keeping His promises when we are in need, but if we try to test God and make Him move on our behalf by asking Him to manipulate our situations on a whim, we blur the line between faith and righteousness. This is always an unacceptable way of testing God. I know there will be times when we may be tempted to doubt God when times get hard, but a true Christian walk always requires faith. Without faith, it is impossible to please God (Hebrews 11:1-3, 6 NKJV). The next time you are tempted to complain to or test God, just take a step back from the mountaintop of temptation or from wandering in the wilderness of wondering and just ask Him to increase your faith and trust in Him instead.

May You Live in Interesting Times

You've probably heard this Chinese proverb quoted, but you may not know its broader context: "May you live in interesting times!"

This sounds at first like a blessing, but it's actually an old Chinese curse. For those who value order, clarity, and stability, "interesting times" may indeed seem like a curse; they are full of ambiguity, crisis, and change. If you enjoy thinking God thoughts and reflecting on permanence, having to expect a new way of living, developing new patterns of behavior, or adjusting to unexpected or unprecedented events, then you may consider it a blessing. Whether you thank God for change or lament over it, there is no doubt that we not only live in interesting times, but we also as Christians, the Church, and society at large face them.

Some characterize our world culture as post-Christian. Whether this is completely accurate or not, it does capture a general sense that the lines of Christian faith have been blurred and suggest that Christianity does not easily mesh with contemporary life. The basic norms of the Christian faith should be grace, love, and service. These norms seem utterly foreign to the rhetoric that shapes our work environments, educational institutions, and politics in most of America. We may identify more with the "values" of merit, competition, and self-interest. These cultural traits have even made their way into religious institutions and churches, I've noticed.

Whether I am speaking with young people or adults, teaching them how to relate their Christian faith to their lives in the wider world is mind-bogglingly difficult. I am discovering that people long for an integrated life of Christian faithfulness but struggle with the blurred lines of a compromised belief system; consequently, they feel deep fragmentation and conflict.

Trusting God When Things Don't Make Sense

Although we feel like the process of integrating Christian faithfulness into our daily life would be complex, the root of the problem is quite simple: we're trying to judge God by our standards. The prevalent misconception is often framed as "if I believe in God, then only good things will happen to me," or "if I am a good person, then only good things will happen to me." If we start from this outlook, when things don't go our way we lose faith. It is almost as if we think we've made some unspoken bargain with God that suggests that we will trust in Him as long as we always get what we want.

WAKE UP! God never promised Christians an easy passage through life. If the lines in this life with God are blurred, it is because we made them so. How we see life matters. How we see God matters even more. There are studies that show consistently that 90 percent of errors we make are due to errors in perception. So, the reasonable conclusion would be to change your perception of God. If you change your perception of God, you can change your reality of God and transform your life. Get into the Word of God on a daily basis. That will help to change your focus on human perception and help you adopt a godly perspective. While perceptions do not have real, effectual power, the Word of God does: "For in it the righteousness of God is revealed from faith to faith" (Rom 1:16 ESV).

Maybe that's why Luke acknowledged the Jews in Berea in the Book of Acts. Paul and Silas were in the synagogue there and noticed something: "these Jews were more noble than those in Thessalonica; they received the word with all eagerness, examining the Scriptures daily to see if these things were so" (Acts 17:11 ESV). Their perception was changed forever by constantly trying to engage with God; so were their souls, because they began to see the mind of God as revealed in Scripture. The more you're exposed to the Word of God, the more the Word of God will begin to remove the blurred lines from your mind and change your perception.

Mankind has been under the invisible sway of Satan for nearly 6,000 years. Under the devil's influence, human beings have set up and organized their own societies, education systems, governments, and even new religions—changing the standards of God based on what seems right to them or suits them. But this has lead only to extreme ideological divides that are rapidly multiplying around this world. Being born in today's world is much like starting a book at its last chapter or sitting down to watch a movie just before the end. If ever there was a time when our world needed a new reality of God, it is now.

God has not been silent about the problems facing humanity—He has been vocal about them from the very beginning, when He was ready to affect change in the world He created. Oddly enough, He always starts the process with one person who is willing to see Him with new eyes and inspire others to do the same. As Mother Teresa said, "I alone cannot change the world, but I can cast a stone across the waters to create many ripples." And I have adopted Doctor Martin Luther King Jr.'s plea as well: "If you want to change the world, pick up your pen and write." In essence, all it takes is one individual doing their part to make a difference in how the world sees God.

If you want to change the world, begin with yourself, and then carry that change into the world one person at a time. What do we possibly have to lose by being willing to change—to see God with new eyes? What is your perception? If our perception of God—how we see God—is as a being full of love, grace, and blessing, a God of second chances, a God who is pulling for us, cheering us on, wanting goodness in our lives, then our reality will be a life of fullness, courage, and hope. He promises a life of taking risks for love, compassion, and peace, a life that is not small but rather one that is lived believing and trusting that with God nothing is impossible. We don't have to bury our head in the sand and hide who we are any longer. There are new experiences waiting to become your new reality. And how exciting is it to think about that reality!

> If you want to change the world, begin with yourself, and then carry that change into the world one person at a time.

CHAPTER 15

THE PARADOX OF CHOICE

Thus, and not otherwise, the world was made.
Either something or nothing must depend on individual choices.
– C. S. Lewis, *Perelandra*

And if it seems evil to you to serve the Lord,
choose for yourselves this day whom you will serve,
whether the gods which your fathers served that were on
the other side of the River, or the gods of the Amorites,
in whose land you dwell. But as for me and my house,
we will serve the Lord.
– Joshua 24:15 (NKJV)

SOME OF THE MOST IMPORTANT truths in life seem impossible on the surface. Experience, however, proves them to be apparent time after time. It isn't until you look a bit deeper, beneath the surface of contradictions, that the real grains of wisdom in some of our most cherished sayings about truth emerge. One of the more interesting contradictions is the paradox of choice. As we begin, I'll provide a bit of detail on the distinction between free will and choice. I hear some pastors, preachers, and even teachers to use the term "free will" often, and I hear mistakes and misuse of the term so often that it has become one of my pet peeves.

Free Will and Free Choice

When you hear the term "free will" used, what the speaker or writer really means is choice or free choice. We generally have

> Choice is usually in conflict with and in defiance of God's *will* in your life.

free choices when we make decisions. Our wills, however, hardly seem free. Christian theology aside, our wills are shaped and influenced by many internal and external factors over the course of our lives. The Bible seems quite clear about the fallen state of our hearts. We basically can't *not* sin, not because we can't *choose* not to sin, but because of our fallen nature and our will *incline* us toward sin. Our choices, then, naturally follow from the intentions of our will.

Even if we could somehow override our wills in our everyday decision-making, such that we didn't break any of the various moral laws, we would certainly fail when it came to the big one: loving God with our whole selves. All the free choices in the world can't fix a will opposed to God. This is why just being a "good" person without choosing to live for God does not satisfy the conditional requirements for salvation. If we won't love God, we almost certainly won't make good choices, no matter how free they may be. Jesus said it this way:

> "If you love Me, keep My commandments. And I will pray the Father, and He will give you another Helper, that He may abide with you forever. . . the Spirit of truth, whom the world cannot receive, because it neither sees Him nor knows Him; but you know Him, for He dwells with you and will be in you."
>
> (John 14:15-17 NHEB)

In the Christian experience, choice is usually in conflict with and in defiance of the *will*. This happens because the *will's* intentions are fixed at a position determined by internal and external carnal influences. Numerous factors go into making choices, which may range from the exceedingly simple to highly complex considerations and varied conditions. The nature of choice is complex—it involves selecting one option and leaving others behind. Letting go of possibilities. It affects how a person evolves, how a relationship with something or someone begins, and if it will end.

In many situations, choice comes naturally. It is what we do every day, all day. But there are times when making a choice requires a lot of intentional forethought, making it intriguing and at times scary. The paradox of choice can be best understood in this sense: when anyone experiences a moment of choice, they find themselves in a real and underexplored phenomenon. Research shows that, the more choices you have, the less satisfied you will be with each one that's available. The theory is that when we have so many options, we have greater opportunity to attach a significant cost factor to selecting any particular one; therefore, we're less happy with our decision—because of the *cost factor*.

> Limitless choice does not actually make us happy.

The Demand for Choice

We make choices for many reasons. We make them with good intentions or because of doubt, convenience, or conviction. We may feel uncomfortable with ambiguity or ambivalence and decide on a safe choice, or we may be brazen enough to try a risky one. Sometimes our minds are divided and we just don't know what to choose.

At the beginning of this chapter, we noticed that Joshua was pushing Israel for a decision. He used an interesting phrase in his discourse with the group of Israelites: "And if it seems evil to you to serve the Lord . . ." The phrase *seems evil* is translated as unjust, unreasonable, or inconvenient. Joshua challenged the people. He said: "You choose!" Underneath his words lies a powerful insinuation. He implies that the worship of God is so highly reasonable, necessary, and beneficial, and the service of idols so absurd, vain, and malignant, that if it were left free for all men to take their choice, every man in his right senses must—needs to—choose the service of God before that of idols. And he provokes them to bind themselves faster to God by their own choice.

Why did the people of God have a difficult time choosing? For the same reason why many are still having trouble choosing God exclusively today. To answer this question, I must address a much simpler question: Why do we have trouble making a choice, period? Herein lies the paradox of choice. A closer look at Israel's situation gives us a clue. Joshua preached the same as his mentor Moses, affirming that man must make a decision to serve God or the world. The message is the same today. Who will you choose? The choice is yours to make. The patriarchs were, as God attests again and again, faithful. However, the people of Israel failed to observe the terms of God's conditional promises to them.

God mandates conditional terms for having a relationship with Him: obedience to His will, commitment to absolute and moral truth, and faithfulness to Him—and Him only. Like Israel, we demand options so we don't feel compelled to make a choice that will lock us in to any one thing, belief, or person. Making a choice represents unquestionable loyalty, and we love to keep our options open. The culture we live in demands choice. God demands choice. But we demand *options*. We imagine that more options mean more freedom. And most people think that limitless freedom must be a good option. The problem with limitless freedom is that it creates the psychological issue of "choice overload." Choice overload is the result of having access to too many options. Decision-making becomes more difficult and less satisfying, even to the point that people might even avoid making an important decision altogether.

God refers to such a person as "double-minded," and warns that such behavior results in "instability in all his ways" (James 1:8). The most miserable Christians I've seen are those who live with a foot in both worlds. They hedge their bets. They have one eye on heaven and one on earth. They call on the name of Christ, but they still try to find security, satisfaction, pleasure, or fulfillment in the things of this world. They're riding the fence. And they're not happy. It is then we drown in the details—by weighing the options. And the more we dig for more options, the more we fear making the wrong decision.

The Irony of Options

The irony of options is that this apparently limitless choice doesn't actually make us happy. The number of choices available to us become overwhelming, and actually make it difficult for us to ever have the joy of committing fully to anything or anyone. Even if we do commit, our culture encourages us to feel dissatisfied with the choice we've made. The freedom of choice turns into a mental and emotional prison—that's the paradox of choices. We must reconcile the illusion of freedom with the reality of confinement.

But there is one thing in particular that is markedly different about our choices when it comes to God. The amazing paradox of Christian freedom is that when we take God-prescribed risks and make God-ordained choices, we don't restrict our freedom, *we increase it!* God calls us to be free of our fears and attachments so that we may have the freedom to accept a full spiritual life. When we choose to cling to our comfort zone, it chains us to indecision and fear, a sign that Satan is trying to prevent us from fully heeding God's call.

Satan does all he can to destroy God's work. He seeks the misery of all mankind. He desires that all men might be miserable, like himself. He does not love us. He does not want anything good for us. He does not want us to be happy. He wants to make us his slaves, and he uses many disguises to try and enslave us. When we follow the temptations of Satan, we limit our discernment of God's reality. This can and will only lead to disillusionment—the illusion of happiness, freedom, control, and a future hope without God. Here are just a few nuggets of God's truth that Satan never, ever wants you to connect with:

God Concerning Satan:

"But I am afraid that just as Eve was deceived by the serpent's cunning, your minds may somehow be led astray from your sincere and pure devotion to Christ."

(2 Corinthians 11:3 NIV)

"You belong to your father, the devil, and you want to carry out your father's desires. He was a murderer from the beginning, not holding to the truth, for there is no truth in him. When he lies, he speaks his native language, for he is a liar and the father of lies."

(John 8:44 NIV)

"The one who does what is sinful is of the devil, because the devil has been sinning from the beginning. The reason the Son of God appeared was to destroy the devil's work."

(1 John 3:8 NIV)

God Concerning Himself:

"Happy is that people, that is in such a case: yea, happy is that people, whose God is the Lord."

(Psalm 144:15 KJV)

"So, if the Son sets you free, you will be free indeed."

(John 8:36 NIV)

"The world is unprincipled. It's dog-eat-dog out there! The world doesn't fight fair. But we don't live or fight our battles that way—never have and never will. The tools of our trade aren't for marketing or manipulation, but they are for demolishing that entire massively corrupt culture. We use our powerful God-tools for smashing warped philosophies, tearing down barriers erected against the truth of God, fitting every loose thought and emotion and impulse into the structure of life shaped by Christ. Our tools are ready at hand for clearing the ground of every obstruction and building lives of obedience into maturity."

(2 Corinthians 10:3-6 MSG)

"For I know the plans I have for you," declares the LORD, "plans to prosper you and not to harm you, plans to give you hope and a future."

(Jeremiah 29:11 NIV)

God's Choice of You

With just a few verses of Scripture, I have offered you options. And now, in the words of Joshua: You choose! You need to choose, because God has already made His choice—God chose you!

In John 15:16 (NIV), Jesus says, "You did not choose me, but I chose you and appointed you so that you might go and bear fruit—fruit that will last—and so that whatever you ask in my name the Father will give you." Ephesians 1:4 (NIV) says, "He chose us in Him before the creation of the world to be holy and blameless in His sight." First Peter 2:9 (NIV) says, "You are a chosen people, a royal priesthood, a holy nation, God's special possession, that you have been given the privilege to declare the praises of Him who called you out of darkness into His wonderful light."

God could have given up on His love affair with mankind. He could have resorted to using brute force to demand our loyalty or given us a kind of spiritual lobotomy that would take away any choice but to love Him. Even now, He could easily obliterate our enemy and demand the allegiance of our hearts. But if God did such a thing, that would annul the love affair that began with the Trinity in Genesis 1:26 (BSB): "Let Us make man in Our image, after Our likeness."

We must recognize this with certainty, because it is undeniable that God has chosen those who are believers in Jesus. But the question is, why? Is there something special about man that led God to choose us? The short answer is no. God did not choose us because of anything inherent in ourselves. Your faith is not the basis of God's choosing you. But it is the result of it. He chose us out of His love and mercy, and for His glory. Revel in this. You carry no burden to measure up to the merit that qualified you for being chosen. There is no such thing.

Man's Choice of God

You will never be all that you can be, and your dreams will never come true as fully as they might, without God in your life. Eric Fellman, President of the Peale Center for Christian Living, put a fine point on the importance of not only man making the right choice, but also making the right changes in life. He said, "There is no more powerful force for positive change in our society than the various incredible effective programs based on the Twelve Steps of Alcoholics Anonymous. Central to every one of these programs is the recognition of the presence of, and the initiation of a search for a relationship with God."[1]

However, a relationship between God and man can only happen if man says "yes." You see, although, God desires a relationship with man, God does not *need* a relationship with man in order to survive. Yet God has given to man the freedom to choose a relationship with Him or to deny that relationship. Some Christians are ineffective in the service of God because they have not totally committed themselves to their choice of God. Their lack of dedication is a sign of resistance to His relationship conditions. They keep a reverence or preference for some things of the world: lust, speaking evil, covetousness, worldliness, etc. These things weigh them down and so they cannot grow properly in the Lord and are consequently useless in His service. The Hebrews writer urges us to "lay aside every weight and the sin which so easily ensnares us" so we can run with endurance, unencumbered by the world (Hebrews 12:1 HCSB).

We must either grasp God completely or the world completely. We will fail if we try to serve both, according to Matthew 6:24 and

1 Kings 18:21. We can deceive ourselves into thinking that we are serving God while our hearts are devoted to the world. We must examine our thoughts and our actions to see if we are bearing fruit to the world or to the Lord. Here is where we have the free will to choose. *Choose wisely.*

CHAPTER 16

BRIDGE OVER TROUBLED WATERS

You might be troubled on every side, yet not distressed.
You might be perplexed, but not in despair.
You might be persecuted, but not forsaken.
You might be cast down, but not destroyed.
— 2 Corinthians 4:8-9 (added emphasis)

"I'LL BE YOUR BRIDGE OVER deep water if you trust in my name." The speaker here is Jesus; the context, his raising of Lazarus from the dead (John 11:32-33). So, whereas we think of a "bridge over troubled waters" today as a message from one friend to another offering help in turbulent times, I am submitting for your consideration the idea that, just as Jesus was a friend of Lazarus, we too can identify Jesus as a friend. He will even stick closer than any brother. He is the one who laid Himself down so that we could cross over rivers of pain without drowning in them.

An Unyielding Foundation

Christians are not exempt from what Shakespeare called "the slings and arrows of outrageous fortune." This metaphor, used by Hamlet, refers to the injuries we might receive in unforeseen situations. Christians are not exempt from Satan's weapons: pains, griefs, and hurts. They come to Christians as to others, and we constantly find ourselves having to swim against what feels like a stream of misfortunes at work, at home, and even in church. How can we prepare ourselves for such traumas? The best we can do is make sure the foundations of our faith are solid, the specifics of it are firmly anchored in our minds, and our habits of devotion and goodwill are as they should be. [1]

> Certainty is the mark of the common-sense life, and gracious uncertainty is the mark of the spiritual life.

For this cause, we faint not because Christ is our bridge over troubled waters, those occasional floods in life that threaten to wash us away. When they hit, struggling against them can push us to the point of exhaustion. When we think we cannot go another inch, when the storms of life arise—and they will—call upon His name. He will come to your aid and calm the storm with a powerful "peace be still." The storm will obey His command. So don't give up and don't give in, because Jesus *will* carry you through. And what He's doesn't carry you through He will be your bridge over—He will be your calm in the storm.

When I was younger, uncertainty used to be crazy scary for me. Living a fear-based existence, I went to great lengths to avoid change and the reality of the unknown. While we are all wired to crave certainty and to feel comfortable when we think we've achieved some sort of stability, it's all an illusion. There's no certainty except God and the uncertainty in this world.

While I still get anxious from time to time when God hints at my unknown future, I also feel a twinge of excitement. Uncertainty and change are essential to growth in any area of life. Life isn't static. It's in a constant state of flux, it flows like a river. As much as I would like to stay in my comfort zone, even if I suspect at times that makes me complacent, I know I have to let go of "what is." The unknown is scary, but, it is also the preferred way for God to bring good things into our lives. Paul writes to the church in Romans and reveals an amazing insight. It completely changed my perspective about life experiences. He writes:

> "And we know that **all things** work together **for good** to them that love God, to them who are the called according to his purpose."
>
> (Romans 8:28 KJV)

After years of practical application of this message from Apostle Paul, I've learned not to judge anything as good *or* bad. Whatever shows up is merely something different or new. We can't begin to judge whether something is "good" or "bad" when it presents itself, because we don't have the capacity to put it into the framework of God's larger plan for our lives. What I do know is that to get from one destination in life to the other along our Christian walk, we have to go through troubled waters. In these waters, there are sometimes predators waiting to sink their teeth into our happiness—piranhas eager to nibble away at your hope for a brighter future. And if you're not careful, they will take you under. It does not matter what your status is in society or how smart you think you are, you cannot travel from destiny's point A to point B on your own strength.

There has to be an unyielding foundation for us to be able to progress from one destination to the next on our spiritual path. God has provided that solid construct in Jesus Christ. He is the foundation on which we stand. He becomes our bridge when we encounter troubled waters.

Certainty in Uncertainty

Humans have a natural inclination to be precise. We are always trying to forecast accurately what will happen next. We look upon uncertainty as a bad thing. But that is not the nature of the spiritual life. The nature of the spiritual life is that we are certain in our uncertainty. Certainty is the mark of the common-sense life, and gracious uncertainty is the mark of the spiritual life. To be certain of God means that we are uncertain in all our ways, not knowing what tomorrow may bring. Jesus confirms this according to gospel of Matthew:

> "Give your entire attention to what God is doing right now, and don't get worked up about what may or may not happen tomorrow. God will help you deal with whatever hard things come up when the time comes."
> (Matthew 6:34 MSG)

When life stares us down with its antagonizing challenges, often, it is not because we are uncertain of God, just uncertain of what He is going to do next. If our certainty is only in our beliefs, we develop a sense of self-righteousness, become overly critical, and are limited by the view that our beliefs are complete and settled. But when we have the right relationship with God, life is full of spontaneous, joyful uncertainty and expectancy. Jesus said, "believe also in Me" (John 14:1), not "believe only certain things about Me."

With every stage of life, even the ones we think we have prepared for, we encounter a degree of uncertainty that can threaten to unravel us. Even in the midst of uncertain circumstances, however, we can always be certain of God. We can be certain that He will be with us, certain that He will walk with us through every difficult step, and certain that as we leave the details of our lives to Him, we will at many times be uncertain about how He will work it all out, but certain that He will. It really comes down to trusting God with our lives. As soon as we abandon ourselves to God and give our entire attention to what He is doing through us now—the assignment in life He has placed closest to us today—He begins to fill our lives with not uncertainty, but divine surprises.

Uncertainties are merely divine surprises in disguise. Apparently uncertain seasons are usually the most powerful God-moments we will ever experience. They often put God on display more than other seasons, demonstrating that God exists, and that He rewards those who seek Him (Hebrews 11:6). So, if you are in one of those dark seasons, take heart. You are likely experiencing what it means to have a God "who acts for those who wait for Him" (Isaiah 64:4 ESV).

While you wait, read scriptural passages that embody spiritual principles applicable to your situation, and live with them. Hold them up as a banner in the presence of any and every form of discord, until such a time as these principles become automatic in your thought life. This is a vital part of "dwelling in the secret place of the Most High" (Psalm 91:1 KJV), "living, moving, and having our being" (Acts 17:28 KJV) continuously in God—the consciousness of God. Not just for a few minutes while reading a book or listening to a sermon or lecture. Despite the demands which are made upon us by the world, we must pause at frequent intervals during the day and during the night to practice being in the presence of God. [2]

Strength in Waiting

Although sometimes you might feel like you are in the waiting room of life, be assured that God has a purpose and a plan for you. Not to worry—

> God's timing is not the same as ours. He sees the big picture, and we see only a snippet.

His timing is perfect. In Him, there is one very important assurance, which is that God strengthens us as we lean on Him during delays. In the book of Isaiah, we are described as an eagle soaring—an apt metaphor for how the believer who abides in the Lord will be lifted and sustained by His Spirit:

> "Have you not known? Have you not heard? The everlasting God, the Lord, the Creator of the ends of the earth, neither faints nor is weary. His understanding is unsearchable. He gives power to the weak, and to those who have no might He increases strength. Even the youths shall faint and be weary, and the young men shall utterly fall, but those who wait on the Lord shall renew their strength; they shall

mount up with wings like eagles, they shall run and not be weary, they shall walk and not faint."

(Isaiah 40:28-31 NKJV)

I don't think any of us like hardships of any kind. Sometimes it seems our troubles or storms last way too long. In the past, I have often indirectly attempted to nudge God in my prayer conversation with Him. I would make innocent statements like: "There's got to be a shorter path, a quicker route to get me on the other side this thing—I'm sure of it." But then I remember, His ways are not like our ways. Within His own reasoning, God chooses to take us on a different route.

There've been times in my life when He's not only changed my path, He kept me in a certain place longer than I would have expected. He orchestrated and precisely altered events that should've taken days and caused them to be delayed for weeks, even months. His divine detours have kept me in difficult places longer than expected—and certainly for longer than I wanted. I found myself saying things like, "If only He'd . . ." and "I wish God would . . ." Has that ever happened to you?

His timing is not the same as ours. He sees the big picture, and we see only a snippet. When He keeps us in the hard places instead of delivering us right away, I believe it's so that we grow to depend on Him more, to mold us and shape us, form us more like His image. The storms teach us patience. They help strengthen our trust and faith, that we would become spiritually mature and sensitive to His calling in our lives.

When Will It Be Over?

God will use what we learn in every trial and storm that we encounter to help us make a mark in this world. The troubles we walk through can bring glory to Him. He will use our lives, the joy and faith we have, in spite of our problems, to draw others to Himself, and to help us to remember that what we see around us is not all there is.

For He has more in store. And it is something greater than we could ever imagine.

But still, we ask ourselves "when will it all be over?". During the storm, we rarely can see its significance or why it has to happen. I think they call that "being human." Isaiah 55:8-9 tells us that His ways are much higher than our ways and His thoughts much higher than our thoughts. As human beings, we won't always know the reason behind how God works in our lives, why He chooses a particular storm for one and not another. We're not expected to know all of the answers. We're only expected to trust Him.

The struggles, troubles, and trials we suffer are always an opportunity for God to reveal His power to us. Each time a painful situation brings you to your knees, use that position to give glory to God! It frustrates the devil when you do. Never let the | People struggle to understand God's rationale in crisis.

enemy convince you to surrender in the turbulent of storms, for you are nowhere near being defeated. You have been made more than a conqueror through Christ, and He is not about to let you go under.

What we *can* be sure of is that no matter how long the waters are troubled or how hard the trial is, He is always working behind the scenes, even when it seems like nothing is happening. He has not forgotten us, nor has He left us. He loves us and constantly concerns Himself with the intricate details and directions of each of our lives. Even when it doesn't feel good, when it hurts more than you can bear, He is diligently executing that which is working out for our good.

Waiting Reveals Two Needs and Two Problems

There are two needs and two problems every believer will face in his or her Christian walk in the world. Just to be human is to deal with emotional and physical pain on a day-to-day basis. This is the practical and existential effect of suffering distress, disappointment, and uncertainty. Even Christians, who confess a living God, may wonder: Where is this God when we need Him? Why doesn't He do something? These questions may lead to doubt, and then to unbelief.

From those who choose to question the existence of God to the atheists who are convinced that there is no God, many see only vindication of their unbelief in events like the 2018 Marjory Stoneman Douglas High School shooting, in Parkland, Florida. Nineteen-year-old Nikolas Cruz confessed to being the perpetrator of the heinous crimes. He was charged with seventeen counts of premeditated murder and seventeen counts of attempted murder. Those who doubt the existence of God or question His reasoning might hear a father or a mother on CNN proclaiming, "It's a miracle that my son or daughter survived," and wonder: Would it have been much bother for God to have saved everyone else?

This is no new argument. People struggle to understand God's rationale in times of crisis or disaster. I have heard it all my life, and I confess there were times I even had the same questions, when tragedy struck close to home. If we consider similar incidents— and worse—that are unfolding around the world and couple it with the academic freedom of the modern secular university system, unbelievers and marginal believers alike are able to turn extensive and deep human suffering against ungrounded faith with devastating effect. Furthermore, they attempt to curry support for the idea that a god who would let such things happen is not a God that most Christians would want to defend. Contrary to these assertions, a Christian's faith in God is not a humiliating emotional crutch, but a source of joy in overcoming the practical and existential problem of suffering the troubled waters in this world. I am confident that true Christians know within themselves that their faith, no matter what, has been a source of strength.

Only by being faithful to God can we attest to the perfect revealing of His protective and redemptive plan through the murky waters of life's many challenges. Despite the severity of our troubling situations and suffering, we must resolve to wait on God. In the meantime, the words of Peter remind us that the Lord "is not slow about His promise, as some count slowness, but is patient toward you, not wishing for any to perish but for all to come to repentance" (2 Peter 3:9, *NASB*). God is "just" (morally right and fair) before us; the only question that remains is: Are we "just" before Him?

If we are, we should take an interest in trying to understand the intellectual and spiritual problem of suffering. When we do, coming successfully through the danger of the emotional side of our problems will take on a divine posture. Emotionalism allow our feelings to interpret our circumstances and form our thoughts about God. So, with this human tendency in mind, I will keep this simple by dealing with two problems "waiting on God" reveals. They are common tactics to distract us from a God-centered response. I will also share with you the two needs that are critical for grounding us in faith

The first problem with troubled waters are troubled hearts. But we should note up front that a troubled heart is really the result of a deeper problem, which we will address later.

The first need is "Let not your heart be troubled." "Troubled" comes from the Greek word *tarassw*. Literally, it means "to agitate, stir up, trouble (a thing, by the movement of its parts to and fro) as with water." Metaphorically, it means "to cause inward commotion,

> God judges the validity of our belief system according to the heart.

take away calmness of mind, disturbing one's poise." Thus, it means "to disquiet, make restless; to strike one's spirit with fear and dread; to render anxious or distressed."

A more modern translation of this verse might be more like, "Do not let your heart be troubled" or "You must not let your heart be troubled." The aspect or action of the verb "not" commands the termination of anyone who is experiencing the problem of a troubled heart, as well as the termination of the continuation of this as a pattern of life. By applying the truth of Scripture, like those given in this passage, we learn that we are to consistently calm the agitation of our hearts. Whenever the disciples were troubled, the Lord was there, calling on them to deal with their fears—not to resist or internalize them.

The second problem, the root of a troubled heart, is fear coupled with unbelief. The greatest problem in an individual's life is not an actual storm, but the fear they carry in them *into* the storm. This fear is caused by an unbelief in God. For many, belief in God is merely a concept, not a reality. All borderline Christians and non-Christians alike share this, and it leads to troubled hearts. Isaiah wrote, "But the wicked *(those who have a disregard for righteousness, truth, honor, and justice)* are like the tossing sea, for it cannot be quiet, and its waters toss up refuse and mud. 'There is no peace,' says the Lord, 'for the wicked'" (Isa. 57:20-21 NIV).

God judges the validity of our belief system according to the heart. Matthew 15:8-9 (NIV) says: "These people honor me with their lips, but their hearts are far from me. They worship me in vain; their teachings are merely human rules." And Jeremiah explores how God validate our faith as well. He states what the Lord says about it: "The heart is deceitful above all things and beyond cure. Who can understand it? I the Lord search the heart and examine the mind" (Jeremiah 17:9-10 NIV).

Because of this misconception, there unfortunately are those who consider themselves Christian yet still harbor a disregard for certain aspects of God-defined righteousness, truth, honor, and justice. They suffer the same discontentment and lack of peace as the unbeliever.

It is here, then, that we find the second need, but this need is one which, when corrected, also becomes the solution. What men need is an authentic relationship with God through earnest belief or faith in God. As the Lord points out, to believe in God is to also believe in Him who is "the way, the truth, and the life." Uncertainty or ignorance or a lack of spiritual understanding about God and His plan weakens our faith. This naturally results in troubled hearts. Even the disciples, who walked closely with Christ for three and a half years, had troubled hearts because of their inability to understand the Word as it related to the sufferings of the Messiah. Though clearly taught in the Old Testament, they had as yet not grasped the need for the cross. They believed in Him as the Messiah, the Son of God, but they were struggling with His repeated comments about His suffering, death, and resurrection.

Likewise, we struggle with the need to experience trials, storms, and troubled waters in life because we lack the full understanding of the Word of God. We need to die for the resurrection of our new life, our destiny, and His purpose in this world through us.

As we boldly take steps into the unknown, we can glean wisdom and advice from the disciples' encounter with storms. Just as He did with the disciples, God intentionally uses life's storms to mature our faith. They make us brave when we have been robbed by fear and left trembling on the side of the road. When we weather the storms in our lives, we learn perseverance. I believe the affirmation found in the book of James:

> "Consider it pure joy, my brothers and sisters, whenever you face trials of many kinds, because you know that the testing of your faith produces perseverance. Let perseverance finish its work so that you may be mature and complete, not lacking anything."
>
> (James 1:2-4 NIV)

Whether it is due to a mass shooting or a charged political climate, this world is constantly morphing towards more instability. If our hope is grounded in the unrest and turbulence around us, we will sink. Ask the Apostle Peter (Luke 8:22-25), and he will tell you that our hope cannot be on the storms of life, but that we must rest in the God who controls the storm.

He will never change, and we can put our trust in Him. In uncertain times, God is a time-tested and proven, solid foundation we can stand on. God is our refuge and strength, an ever-present help in trouble. He is our bridge over troubled waters.

CHAPTER 17

BACK WHERE YOU BELONG

True belonging only happens when we present our authentic,
imperfect selves to God. Our sense of belonging can never
be greater than our level of self-acceptance—I belong.
I belong to Him and He belongs to me.
We have become one.

— the author

AS WE COME TO THE conclusion of our time together, you should be aware that life as a Christian can be quite an adventure. If you are familiar with J. R. R. Tolkien's best-selling novel and blockbuster movie trilogy based on *The Lord of the Rings*, you'll be able to make a parallel between our Christian adventure and Frodo Baggins and Samwise Gamgee's. You may progress from hiking along a proverbial treacherous mountain trail, to braving a fierce storm, to battling the enemy, to sailing on a placid lake to strolling through a pleasant field.

There are ups, downs, and unexpected turns in life. Though you may go back along a trail you have been traveling, the one thing you don't want during your Christian walk is to go backward spiritually—straying out of alignment with God's will. The truth is that we can rarely know exactly what God's will is in any given situation anyway. We probably veer off His path of perfect love way more often than we realize. Our lapse may be a relatively minor one, and unintentional. Sometimes it may be simply falling back through neglect by not praying, reading the Bible, or keeping your focus on living for God.

On the other hand, a believer may depart from God deliberately, choosing to indulge in this life's sinful pleasures. This type of separation can carry disastrous consequences. It can bring dishonor to the One who laid down His life for us, Jesus Christ. It can also sadden and bring grief to the lives of our loved ones. Of course, disconnection from God can bring turmoil into the believer's own life as well. He may be plagued by guilt or even a feeling of despair or condemnation. You might even begin to think, "Is there still a place for me in God's grand plan?" No matter what journey you may have found yourself on in life, God *will* continue to call you back into a relationship with Him.

But, as William Hines puts it, God wants you to love Him—His way. The love of God involves nothing less than your whole person. We love Him by first making the decision to do so and then by devoting all that we are to the task of loving Him. Loving God does not mean that we have to avoid pleasant experiences, nor, conversely, does it mean we can do only those things that we want to do and assume that He will always protect us from discomfort or harm. It does mean that we must not participate in sin, and that what we do we do with the express purpose of bringing honor to the Lord. The goal is to love God across the whole spectrum of our lives. [1]

There are five keys I want to submit for your consideration that will facilitate your return to an authentic relationship with God and help to align you with His will for your life.

First Key: Acknowledge to Yourself and God Where You Are

"And the LORD God called unto Adam, and said unto him, Where art thou?" (Genesis 3:9 KJV). The Lord God knew right where Adam was, so why would He ask that question? Nothing is hidden from God's sight. God, in His omniscience, knew exactly where Adam was hiding and why he was hiding: "The eyes of the LORD are in every place, beholding the evil and the good" (Proverbs 15:3 KJV). By asking, "Adam, where art thou?" the Lord was bringing Adam to a place of accountability. Adam is forced to confess that he is hiding from God because he has blatantly disobeyed God's commandment.

God was prompting thoughts in Adam's mind. He was provoking Adam to acknowledge and take responsibility for the spiritual disconnect. Upon hearing God's voice, Adam immediately thought (Genesis 3:7-10 paraphrased), "I should be fellowshipping with Him. I should be right by His side, but look at me, fearful and hiding amongst the trees! My relationship with Him is severed!" Adam had to acknowledge to himself and to God that there had been a shift in his obedience and loyalty.

> Prayer is a privilege by which we are enabled by God's Spirit to move ourselves toward His will.

Acknowledgment is a starting point for self-discovery. There is a particular incident in King David's life that illustrates the importance of acknowledging a sin or a disconnect to God and yourself. If you consider the far-reaching effects of David's adultery and murder, it seems that his sin was against not only himself but many others: Bathsheba, Uriah, Israel, etc. Ultimately, David realized that His sin was against Holy God, the one who is justified in His words and blameless in His judgments. God, not the ones against whom David sinned, would be the One before whom David would have to give an account and face judgment.

There are many lessons we can lesson from this one incident. But it is important not to overlook the numbing effect David's sin had upon his own heart. His confession came about one year after his sin. Like many of us, he had managed to excuse himself for his sin throughout that time. In fact, he was ready to put to death the man described in Nathan's story (2 Sam. 12:5, ESV), until he heard the dreaded words, "You are the man!" David's sin numbed his heart and separated him from God. God took the initiative to confront David in his sin and call David to repentance—to the place in God where he belongs.

Do you find it easy to justify offenses in your life? Are you satisfied with the state of your relationship with God? Deep down, on the inside of you, is there a nagging unrest about your soul that is telling you that something is amiss in your relationship with God? Listen to what happened next with David. The realities God led David to recognize in verses 3-6 are what caused David to cry out for God's mercy in verses 1-2, and later in verses 7 and following. Because David was a sinner by nature and choice, and because he had actually sinned against the holy and just God, his only hope for redemption was for God to show him mercy.

Like us, David could not erase his own sin. He therefore called upon God to "blot out" his transgressions, "wash" him of his iniquities, and "cleanse" him of his sin. Why did David believe God would hear his appeal and respond in such a way? Because God is steadfast in love and abundant in mercy. As fallen humans, we stockpile an arsenal of countless ways, reasons, and excuses to avoid confronting the most difficult issues in life. We attempt to avoid overcoming them and allowing God to form and shape us into His image. If we could only remember that bringing God into the picture unleashes forces that will not only help us to overcome, but will also protect us from the pitfalls that litter our path toward right alignment with His will!

Perhaps it isn't that you have wandered away from God or that you have committed some great sin. Yet, with all the knowledge of God you may have, you may still seem to feel emptiness. Maybe you are looking for more out of life. Are you frustrated because you know there is more to the abundant life He has to offer than you are experiencing? Maybe you're standing in the middle of a broken life and you don't know what to do or where to go to pick up the pieces. These are the questions many of us have, or have had, at some point in life.

We question because we desperately want answers. We desperately need to see the light in the midst of our own confusion. However, I think there is a significant difference between questioning that brings wisdom and a higher understanding of God and the kind of questioning that simply seeks to validate man and man's ways. The key to questioning God is to approach Him with the purpose of understanding and making adjustments for proper alignment with His plan for us.

Second Key: Align Your Will with God's Will

There are times when we feel like God is confining us and shutting doors we wish we could open. We pray. We plead. We cry, "Please, God." But to no avail. Usually we are too busy complaining to hear His reassuring voice: "For God is working in you, giving you the desire and the power to do what pleases him" (Philippians 2:13 NLT). In essence, He has something amazing in mind for us, and it is in accordance with His will. Trust Him. It's not that God isn't answering our prayers. He just has something better in mind for us. Something wonderful we can't even imagine.

We can either struggle with Him, question His motives, and plead for our own desires, or we can pray, trust His motives, and listen to His heart. The purpose of prayer is not to argue with God or to try to persuade Him to move things according to our will. Prayer is a privilege by which we are enabled by God's Spirit to move ourselves toward His will. Now, there is a difference between God's "will" and His purpose. God's will has been established, but God's purpose can only be discovered as He reveals it.

Most people think of God's will as something we can find if we just look hard enough, or as the receiving of clear guidance from God when we're making decisions. We assume that if we just knew what God wanted, we'd do it. Too often, however, the problem is not that we don't *know* what God desires for our lives, but that *we just don't want to do what we already know He wants*. Sometimes, though, we try to live the Christian life out of sheer self-determination and grit, only to discover that our will is not sufficient to sustain us.

Staying aligned with God, being in step with His will, being in unity with the Spirit—these all mean that we are coming back to the place in God where we belong. As a Christian, you only fall out of alignment with God when you embrace rebellion at the level of your soul.

Alignment is a very simple concept that has to do with your soul's attitude towards God. At any moment in time, you either sincerely care about pleasing Him, or you do not. If you do, then you are in alignment with Him. Alignment is not about behavior only, nor is it undone by sin. You can be aligned with God in your soul and still sin with your body. In these cases, you will not enjoy sin—your flesh might enjoy it, but inside your soul will be groaning in repulsion. This is how you know that you are not obeying the will of God, even though your soul has been sealed by God through Christ. Notice a section of the Apostle Paul's letter to the Church at Ephesus:

> "And grieve not the holy Spirit of God, **whereby ye are sealed unto the day of redemption**. Let all bitterness, and wrath, and anger, and clamour, and evil speaking, be put away from you, with all malice: And be ye kind one to another, tenderhearted, forgiving one another, even as God for Christ's sake hath forgiven you."
>
> (Ephesians 4:30-32 KJV)

Third Key: Identify with Who God Says You Are

I have always said that you will never get a revelation about who you are in God until God determines that

> Don't live by your own power or understanding.

you are ready to hear it. Here is a historical case in point. The Pharisees and Sadducees came and demanded that Jesus show them a sign from heaven (Matthew 16:1). Jesus responded, "A wicked and adulterous generation seeketh after a sign; and there shall no sign be given unto it, but the sign of the prophet Jonas" (Matthew 16:4 KJV). "Later, Jesus called His disciples together and asked: Whom say ye that I am? And Simon Peter answered and said, Thou art the Christ, the Son of the living God" (Matthew 16:15-16 KJV).

Notice Jesus's response: "Blessed art thou, Simon Barjona: for flesh and blood hath not revealed it unto thee, but my Father which is in heaven" (Matthew 16:17 KJV). Christ was saying, you didn't get this revelation just by walking with Me, Peter. My Father revealed it to you from heaven, not just because you asked, but because you were ready to receive the message. In short, Peter received the amazing, initial revelation that comes to everyone who believes. When you are ready to believe, then you are ready to receive.

Yet, elsewhere we read: "Then charged he his disciples that they should tell no man that he was Jesus the Christ" (Matthew 16:20 KJV). Why? Why would Jesus do that? Hadn't heaven itself already announced that He was the Lamb of God who had come to save the world?

The fact is, the disciples weren't ready to testify that He was the Messiah. You see, readiness is key to revelation. Their revelation of Him was incomplete. They knew nothing of the cross, the way of suffering, the depths of their Christ's sacrifice. Okay, yes, they had already healed the sick. Yes, they cast out devils and witnessed to many. But even though they had been with Jesus for those years, they still had no deep, personal revelation of who He was. They were, in fact, comingling the opinions of others concerning who Jesus was, until God gave Peter the revelation:

> "They replied, 'Some say John the Baptist; others say Elijah; and still others, Jeremiah or one of the prophets' 'But what about you?' he asked. 'Who do you say I am?' Simon Peter answered, 'You are the Messiah, the Son of the living God.' Jesus replied, 'Blessed are you.'"
>
> (Matthew 16: 14-17 KJV)

We all want to know who we are. We seek and search and try to "find ourselves" through others. Many of us have taken personality tests and other assessments to learn more about ourselves. During my graduate studies for my PhD, I had to study human behavior, so I was trained to administer personality-assessment tests. A requisite of the class was that we were to partner with a classmate to administer, analyze, and review our assessment of each other. The results were quite revealing. But I discovered that, as helpful as those tests can be, they still can't answer the question, "What does God think about me? Who does He say that I am?"

In all my years as a Christian, I had never asked the question quite that way until I was at a place in my life years ago where God knew I could truly hear Him. And what I found is that God has a lot to say about what He thinks about us—He has a whole Bible full of opinions. It was there in the Bible all along. If I could summarize it in a short space, here is what it might boil to—We are made in the image of God! Let that sink in. "So God created man in His own image; in the image of God He created him; male and female He created them" (Genesis 1:27 NKJV).

A flower cannot produce a dog, they weren't created in the same likeness. A flower can only reproduce a flower. John 1:12 says, "To all who believed him and accepted him, he gave the right to become children of God." You and I are the children of God! We are made like our heavenly Father. I know that may sound too simple but sometimes, simple truths are the most profound. Life doesn't need to be complex. With the help of God and His Word, we can know who we are and why we're here! Consider these three nuggets of truth:

> *You Are Valuable.*
> My eyes saw your unformed substance (Psalm 139:16). I knit you together in your mother's womb (Psalm 139:13). You are fearfully and wonderfully made (Psalm 139:14). You are more valuable than many sparrows (Matthew 10:31). I have crowned you with glory and honor as the pinnacle and final act of the six days of creation (Psalm 8:5; Genesis 1:26).

> *You Are New.*
> All your sins are forgiven (1 John 1:9). All your unrighteousness has been cleansed by the blood of Jesus (1 John 1:7, 9). You are now righteous in my

sight with the very righteousness of my perfect Son
(Romans 4:5). You've been saved by grace (Ephesians
2:8). You've been justified by faith (Romans 5:1). You
are utterly secure in me; nothing will be able to separate
you from my love in Christ Jesus (Romans 8:39). And
I will never leave you nor forsake you (Hebrews 13:5).

You are My Family and Have My Spirit.
You not only have a new Father, but also a new family
of brothers and sisters (Luke 8:21). You are now part
of the people of God (1 Peter 2:9). And together the
life you now live is by faith in my Son (Galatians
2:20). Look to Jesus. Keep your eyes on him. He is
the author and perfecter of your faith (Hebrews 12:2).

God's purpose in giving us our identity was not so that we would
focus on trying to achieve a sense of superiority. Our identity is for
the sake of making known God's identity. You are God's *masterpiece*
(NLT)—*workmanship* NKJV (Ephesians 2:10). A masterpiece is
defined as "a person's greatest work of art," or a "consummate example
of skill or excellence." Now, when God's Word describes you as His
masterpiece, it is referring to His assessment of you, not what you
think, nor what others think.

But beware, like most masterpieces in the wrong hands, we are
subject to having our identity stolen or faked.

Fourth Key: Discover God's Reason for Why You Are

Perhaps one of the most beautiful and life-affirming passages in the
Bible are the words of David in Psalm:

"My frame was not hidden from You, when I was
made in secret, and skillfully wrought in the lowest
parts of the earth. Your eyes saw my substance, being
yet unformed. And in Your book, they all are written,

the days fashioned for me, when as yet there were none of them."

(Psalm 139:15-16 NASB)

Paul also wrote about God's reason for why you are: "Just as He chose us in Him before the foundation of the world, that we should be holy and without blame before Him in love" (Ephesians 1:4 NASB). God has carefully and individually made each of us, "fearfully and wonderfully" (Psalm 139:14 NSAB). So, if He thought of us and created each of us so intentionally, we need to understand His purpose for the lives He has given us.

King David asked essentially the same question: Why am I here? "When I consider your heavens, the work of your fingers. . . what is man that you are mindful of him, the son of man that you care for him?" (Psalm 8:3-4 NSAB).

If God were to give you the answer to this question, it would be simple, yet profoundly humbling. He would simply say, "Because I want you to represent Me."

"Therefore, walk in a manner worthy of your calling" (Ephesians 4:1). "You are no longer darkness, but light in my Son. Walk as children of light" (Ephesians 5:8). "You are the light of the world, a city set on a hill" (Matthew 5:14). "I have called you" (2 Peter 1:3). "I have chosen you" (Revelation 17:14). "You are now a saint, a servant, a steward, and a soldier" (Romans 1:7; Acts 26:16; 1 Peter 4:10; 2 Timothy 2:3). "You are a witness and a worker" (Acts 1:8; Ephesians 2:10). "Through Jesus you are victorious" (1 Corinthians 15:57). "You have a glorious future" (Romans 8:18). "You are a citizen of heaven" (Philippians 3:20). "You are an ambassador for my Son" (2 Corinthians 5:20).

"We were foreknown and predestined to conform to the image of Jesus" (Romans 8:29-30) God's desire for us is that we gain divine nature, which is eternal life. We are to overcome all sin, and in that process build the body of Christ, the church, which will be to His glory both on earth and for all eternity. This is the very reason that He formed us so fearfully and wonderfully.

There is no time to waste time doing our own will. We are here to do God's will, and to do that we need to be extremely humble, acknowledge our weaknesses as human beings, and go to the "throne of grace to get the help we need to overcome sin" as

> There is no time to waste time doing our own will.

God intended and promised (Hebrews 4:16). The Holy Spirit who led Jesus through His flesh will also lead us through ours. That's why it is written in Romans 8:28:

> "And we know that all things work together for good to those who love God, to those who are the called according to His purpose."
>
> (Romans 8:28 KJV)

In His purpose there is not only a sense of belonging, but a sense of responsibility. Williams Arthur Ward may have said it best:

Do more than belong: participate. Do more than care: help.
Do more than believe: practice. Do more than be fair: be kind.
Do more than forgive: forget. Do more than dream: work.

Fifth Key: Allow God's Transformation and Adjust Your Habits

Genuine transformation is God-achieved and God-sustained, but we must adjust our external habits to align with God's internal mind renewal and transformation process. This is the essence of living by faith—knowing the truth with absolute certainty and walking in the Spirit. As the Apostle Paul said, "I no longer live, but Christ lives in me. The life I now live in the body, I live by faith in the Son of God" (Gal. 2:20 HCSB). As you can see, it is not just about accumulating Bible knowledge, although this has value in and of itself. Increasing knowledge may make one smarter, but knowledge alone cannot transform an individual.

Mind renewal that produces transformation is a work of God in the same way that the salvation of a soul is a work of God. Transformation is a work of the Holy Spirit. He illuminates the truth we already know intellectually, which results in a change in our belief and behavior. But before any God-transformation can take place, it requires that we must first desire a spiritual change. We need to ask ourselves: Do I really want to change, or am I content to remain as I am? How important is it to me to be like Jesus? What price am I willing to pay to be godly?

His word says: "Do not conform to the pattern of this world, but be transformed by the renewing of your mind. Then you will be able to test and approve what God's will is—his good, pleasing and perfect will" (Romans 12:2 NIV). By renewing your mind in God's word, you will be able to test His word through adjusting your habits. This will help to keep you focused and remain in God's will.

How did Jesus stay focused on His mission? We believe that it was because of His habits. Habits are behaviors and actions that we do instinctively, often without much thought. Jesus's habits, His spiritual disciplines, however, were something that He practiced as a regular part of His daily life. So, if we learn from His example, we must also practice discipline in our daily lives.

The habits that Jesus practiced—spending time in solitude and prayer, applying God's Word, abiding in God's unconditional love, and maintaining supportive relationships—kept His life and leadership perfectly aligned with the Father and His mission. God uses our habits (spiritual disciplines) to put us into a place where He can work within us to transform us into the chosen, anointed people that He wants us to become.

Practicing these habits aligns your life and your assignment in life, keeping you on course much like the alignment of your car's tires keeps your car headed in the right direction. When your car is "out of alignment," the tires or wheels that are not aligned properly will pull or steer the car in a different direction from that of the others, and from the way you're trying to go. If you are not careful while you are driving, your car might veer over into another lane or even run off the road into a ditch.

Through our habits, God continually realigns and transforms our life so that our heart, head, and hands remain focused on the purpose and mission that God has given to us. Practicing good habits on a daily basis prevents us from losing our direction and keeps us out of the "ditches" that Satan puts in our way while helping us become a servant who represents God in this world, like Jesus did.

Back Where You Belong

Unlike Jesus, sin still lingers in us. The "things of man" desires mix with "things of God" desires in us. If we are not careful, this can turn our dreams of entering the Kingdom of God into Satanic diversions. The ultimate issue in life is what or whom we worship. The process of true change takes place within us as we are weaned from our love and worship of self, pleasure, and this world; only after this happens can our hearts become wholly devoted to Christ.

May our spiritual change flow out of an intimate relationship with Jesus. We want to please those we love, and we are grieved when we offend them. May we love Jesus, so that our motivation to obey Him will be greater and we will make the choices that only please Him. So, let this be our prayer:

> *Whatever it takes, Lord, align my desires with yours, so that my dreams align with your purposes. Let your will be done through me. Because I'm back. I am back home, where I belong.*

AFTERWORD

Never allow your emotions to cloud your sense of reasoning.
Otherwise, you will always make wrong choices.

~ Clement Ogedegbe

As I conclude this manuscript, I have to say, it has been an exciting exploration and introspective journey. Developing each chapter in *God's Unreasonable Reasoning* was a poignant reminder of the dilemma we face in not only Christendom, but in the world at large. In writing this book, I wanted to reveal why many people have misunderstandings of faith and why they also have misunderstandings of reason. Reason is a tool that God has given us to allow us to draw conclusions and inferences from other information, such as the information He has given us in His Word. Reason is an essential part of Christianity; God tells us to reason (Isaiah 1:18) as the apostle Paul did (Acts 17:17).

Some Christians believe that faith and reason are in conflict, divided by some unbridgeable chasm. They think that one takes over where the other leaves off. In reality, faith and reason work together seamlessly to help us know and love God. In fact, I would not know whether I had been saved unless I used my reason. After all, the Bible nowhere says that "Doctor Williams is saved." Instead it tells me "if you confess with your mouth the Lord Jesus and believe in your heart that God has raised Him from the dead, you will be saved" (Romans 10:9). I have genuinely acknowledged that Jesus is Lord, and I believe that God raised Him from the dead. Therefore, I am saved. I must use logical reasoning to draw this conclusion.

We must demonstrate good reasons for believing what we believe, and we are called to be always ready to share that reason with other people (1 Peter 3:15). So, part of our duty as Christians is to attempt to show unbelievers that our belief in the Scriptures is reasonable, justified, and logically defensible. The Bible makes sense.

This is perfectly appropriate, and this is the kind of reasoning God expects us to use. We are to use logic

> Reasoning with God does not mean arguing with Him or making excuses for ourselves or our actions.

based on the principles of His Word. But human reasoning should never be used to fight *against* God. There have been questions about how we use reason, such as: Can a weak and mortal man or woman influence God? Can we change His mind? Is it wrong to reason with Him?

Contrary to many people's first reaction, God actually urges us to engage with him in conversations about reason: "Come now, and let us reason together" (Isaiah 1:18). Abraham reasoned with God concerning the city of Sodom, and as a result God promised He would not destroy it if just ten righteous people lived there. Moses reasoned with God concerning the rebellious Israelites. God wanted to destroy them for their idolatry, but changed His mind because of Moses's intercession.

Reasoning with God does not mean arguing with Him or making excuses for ourselves or our actions. Nor does it mean trying to get God to change His laws. Reasoning with Him means giving Him reasons for why we're asking for the things we do. God wants us to reason with Him! When we give Him sound, spiritual reasons for our requests, He can gauge very accurately our growth in grace and knowledge. He can also see plainly if we are still carnal and self-centered when our reasoning is in opposition to the principles of His word. People misuse reason when they frame their worldview apart from God's Word. This can involve either treating reason as its own ultimate standard—in other words, as a replacement for God's Word—or tossing it aside as irrelevant to faith.

Neither of these positions is biblical. We are never to attempt to reason in opposition to the Word of God. That is to say, we are not to treat God's Word as a mere hypothesis, as if we can disprove it with our fallible understanding of the universe. We are never to reason in such an absurd, sinful way. Instead, we are supposed to reason from God's Word, taking it as our ultimate unquestionable starting point. Any alternative is arbitrary and self-refuting. Reason is not a substitute for God; rather, it is a gift from God.

The world today is full of people who build on their own theories, who say in their hearts, "God doesn't really mean this or that," who take no heed of the requirements of God, who depend on human reason. These people have been deceived by Satan. Satan's deceptions follow many routes. As we approach the end of time, Satan will make a determined effort to deceive everyone. He has already succeeded in deceiving masses, from the beginning of time. We must be continually on the alert, well grounded in the truth, and fully acquainted with the Scriptures. Satan perverts the truth into a lie, making it appear that God is unreasonable, a sadist. God's guidance doesn't always make sense from a human point of view. People in the world and even a few of us Christians won't always understand the choices God leads us to make.

In fact, it may feel as if you're making a foolish decision when you follow the will of God. But God does not require us to understand His will, just obey it, even if it seems unreasonable. What we must keep in mind is that God knows us better than we know ourselves. The first thing I think of as an example of this is how well Abraham communicates with God. How clearly God can manifest Himself and His will to Abraham. This is why Abraham is called the father of our faith. Abraham believed in God. Abraham believed in God's promise to make of him a great nation, even in the face of the heart-wrenching moment when God commands him to take the life of his only son—the means by which God's promise to Abraham would be kept.

God could command Abraham to offer up his son Isaac because He already knew Abraham had full faith and trust in Him. God could command Abraham to do what seemed unreasonable because God knew that, at the appropriate time, Abraham would also hear the voice of a messenger saying; "Do no lay a hand on the boy. . . Do not do anything to him. Now I know that you fear God, because have not withheld from me your son, your only one" (Genesis 22:10-12 NIV).

To understand that God's plan for our lives is probably not what we would have chosen ourselves is to realize that He is always thinking farther ahead than we are. He's thinking about the blessings and fruit that will come from our lives, while we often think about our security or our significance. God is more concerned with your life than you can possibly imagine. He wants you to truly entrust your life into His good, perfect, and pleasing will. Although we may never fully realize His purposes, if God is unreasonable to us, He is unreasonable in the most wonderful ways ever.

Nothing can compare to the joys of discovering and following the Father's plan for your life. Obey God and leave all the consequences to Him—even when His plans seem a little foolish in human terms.

"The LORD will work out his plans for my life
for your faithful love,
O LORD, endures forever.
Don't abandon me, for you made me."
(Psalm 138:8 NLT)

Bonus Chapter

Because I consider this book to be the sequel to my last book *The God of How*, I would like to include excerpts from Chapter 14, which is entitled: *Behind the Curtain of Cause (A Tapestry of Experiences)*.

Excerpt: *The God of How*

Behind the Curtain of Cause (A Tapestry of Experience)

Journalizing William Jamison II's life experiences was much like walking with a ghost. It was a journey through a mysterious wilderness with no guide to direct the next steps of the sightseer. There were so many experiences that contributed to the shaping of his life, choosing only a few was most difficult. However, behind each story lie the mystery that bares the question of what fueled the cause for each dilemma or situation. Cause, to understand it, one must implore its companion "effect." Cause and effect notes the relationship between actions and events such that one or more are the result of the other or others. Simply stated, a cause is "Why" something happens, and the effect is "What" happens. Behind the curtain of cause lies the enigmatic motive of creation, purpose—God's overall intention or His predetermined, inevitable, irresistible, course of events to fulfill a divine plan.

In His master plan for creation, there are volumes of books that chronicles His plans. Every individual born in this world has his own book in the volume of books. This personalized book of yours has a unique and detailed plan for your reason to be born. Jesus revealed this part of creation's mystery when, in a conversation with God—His Father, He said:

> *Therefore, when he came into the world, He said, Sacrifice and offering You did not desire, but a body You have prepared for Me: In burnt offerings and sacrifices for sin You had no pleasure. Then I said, Behold, I have come—in the **volume of the book** it is written of Me, to do Your will, O God.* (Hebrews 10:5-7 NKJV)

If that wasn't enough insight to inspire you or at the very least, to make you feel some level of personal value to God, here is another slice of truth. God Himself says, *the counsel of the Lord stands forever, the plans of His heart to all generations* (Psalms 33:11 NKJV). Every generation of people that have ever lived and that will ever be born, come into this world with a book written in heaven. Hence, every experience in the world have a predetermined outcome also recorded. Because every human has been given the gift of "free will," we have the proclivity toward choosing to operate either inside or outside the *will* of God; which mean, you will either live in God's perfect will or if you choose to—you can exist in His permitted will.

This is a very involved theological concept, but I have given you enough to understand that absolutely nothing in life is an arbitrary crap shoot. There is a God, and He has an intentional progressive plan for all of His creation.

> A cause is *why* something happens. An effect is *what* happens.

Every experience allowed in our lives have a general divine purpose of keeping or getting us back on track with God's intention for us. There is a deeper more profound purpose, but that is between you and God. In His own timing, He will reveal it to you.

Marcus Aurelius Antonius Augustus, Emperor of the Roman Empire from 161 to his death in 180, said, "What we do now echoes in eternity." I'm not sure if the Emperor understood the depth and far reaching implications of his statement, but it was validated by John, the Revelator. He wrote:

> *And I saw the dead, small and great, standing before God; and the books were opened: and another book was opened, which is **the Book** of Life: and the dead were judged according to their works, by the things which were written in the books.* (Revelation 20:12 NKJV)

The sum total of your experiences and what you accomplish or not, will be weighed and balanced by what God has written in His book concerning you and your purpose.

It bares to reason that if we don't know and understand these theological trues, the experiences we go through will at times seem so wasteful and unnecessary. We are left with this tiresome feeling that questions the *why* of life. When there is a lack of understanding *why* we go through *what* we go through it is a recipe for frustration. Sometimes the frustration of life is so burdensome that we're tempted to curse the day we were born. Remember Job? He was an Old Testament patriarch, who understood such feelings. Amid his personal turmoil, he said to God:

> *Let the day perish wherein I was born, and the night in which it was said, there is a man child conceived.* (Job 3:3 NKJV)

Job could relate to our need to make sense out of what is seemingly nonsense. The search for understanding life's rollercoaster of events are endless and, in many cases, even unsuccessful. Like the dry, dusty throat of a thirsty man lost in a desert, we reach for so many solutions and philosophies that we suppose will quench this thirst. To our dismay, we find ourselves drinking the dust of disillusionment. Empty and discouraged, we throw up our hands in defeat and resort to merely existing in this life. Herein lies the inevitable birthing of the attitude *que sera, sera*, whatever will be, will be. In theological circles, this attitude and philosophy is known as fatalism.

For almost a decade of William's life after his divorce from his wife and resignation of his ministry from the religious denomination with whom he held ministry credentials, this was the way he saw himself. For the first time in his life he would have no denomination to cover and support his future in ministry, no family name to depend upon, and no hopes of growing old with the mother of his children and celebrating the traditional fiftieth year wedding anniversary. All he was left with in the world was his relationship and hope in God. Looking back at it all, this was exactly where God needed William in order to fulfill His purpose in his life. William never saw these unfortunate details of his life coming, but it was written.

Unfortunately, William fell prey to thinking that all his efforts didn't matter. He felt as if he was assigned to a certain fate that would disqualify him from God's original plans in ministry. Each night he prayed that such a fate would not befall him. Thinking this way is a recipe for frustration. So often, we set a course for ourselves, only to veer off toward places we never intended—or worse, come to a stand-still we can't seem to shake. Then, it's only natural to wonder if we've either missed God's best for our lives, or just never saw it clearly to begin with. I'm here to tell you that it is not too late. God hasn't given up on you. He hasn't taken your destiny and given it to someone more worthy.

Here in lies the fault with the philosophy of fatalism, it does not encourage understanding, nor does it enforce the pursuit of purpose. Fatalism implies that we are all subject to life without the benefit of personal choice, life without our cooperation and the intentional pursuit of purpose.

Purpose is best known as one's destiny. To understand destiny is to embrace the fact that your life has been predetermined or predestined. Each of us has a God-given purpose. God has destiny in mind for us. Its potential echoes now and for eternity. It reconciles mankind back to its Heavenly Father. Our God-given purpose meets a God-sized need. It calls us to a destiny that God wrote on our hearts before the creation of time.[2]

When you embrace this fact, you must also embrace the fact that nothing occurs in life without reason or purpose. Without proper direction, we live our lives never knowing the purpose or reason for our experiences, whether good or bad. Knowing and understanding the reason for these experiences will ease the pressures of life and place all events, good or bad, in their proper perspective. Proper perspective may be defined as *the view in which an idea or experience fits that brings completeness, ease, and understanding.*

Perspective, therefore, must be indorsed by a legitimate source of understanding that is based on truth before it can be considered *proper*. Not every perspective is proper, especially in our search for the *why* of life. The most common mistake made by the seekers of truth and meaning is to look for the answers to the questions in life from life itself. The key to understanding life is not in life itself, but in the source of life—God. So, our search should begin with understanding the source of life, for in this search, we will understand the origin and purpose of life.

Behind the curtain of "cause" everything that exists has a beginning, and since it has a beginning, then it is safe to assume that there was an intended purpose. Purpose began as an idea in the mind of God, the source. A plan for the idea was laid and then initiated. But before the idea, plan, and the purpose, there existed something much more important, the void. The void can be described as emptiness or need. In his book, *Northern Memoirs*, Richard Franck said, "Necessity is the mother of invention." Or to paraphrase, necessity gives birth to creation. Therefore, everything that is, is because of something or someone that exists, but is incomplete, invalid, or unresolved (necessity).

If we apply these statements to life, it will be clear that life can be understood only through the source of life and that if life was given, there was first a need or a void to

> When there is a lack of understanding the reason *why* we go through *what* we go through, the experience becomes a recipe for frustration.

be filled. After this, *the idea* of you came into the scheme of eternal planning as the means to which the need will be filled. This need, in turn, created the purpose for your existence. The plan of God represents the course upon which all events will take place. In essence, it is the road that you must travel that will prepare, shape, and define you for your purpose.

In the beginning, it was inconceivable for William to understand how God would use the conflicts of his ministry and marriage to fulfill a higher purpose in his life. He was ostracized by his peers in ministry, restricted from preaching in denominational churches where he frequented and had annual standing invitations. He was told, and even in some cases, it was prophesied that his leaving would yield an unfruitful ministry and that his life would be cursed if he didn't return to the denominational covering. Needless to say, God knew what He had in mind for William; plans to prepare him beyond the limitations and control of a denomination and to give him a hope and an expected end that could not have been achieved where he was, at that time.

Let me take a moment at this point to share an important truth. One that I hope will free others as I have been freed in my past experiences. I have discovered in my relationship with God and through my trials in life that not all prophesy is from God and not every word spoken is anointed. I had to learn the hard way that religious people will at times confuse spiritual discernment with being carnally suspicious, and they will impose their personal convictions on others by clandestinely inserting the phrase that "God spoke to their spirit" as a precursor to their "Word from the Lord." Now, I am a firm believer in spiritual gifts, and I know that God will use individuals as messengers and vessels of impartation, utterances of correction, judgment, and blessings. My statements above are intended for those individuals who abuse spiritual gifts and who use God's name in vain for their own personal agendas. These individuals, if allowed, could hinder your pursuit of God's ultimate purpose for your life. So be careful and discerning about who you allow to speak into your life. As the Scriptures advises us:

Beloved, do not believe every spirit, but test the spirits to see whether they are from God, for many false prophets have gone out into the world. (1 John 4:1 ASV)

The Pursuit of Purpose Is a Continuum

Your pursuit of purpose is a vital element to how you view your experiences. I embrace the concept that this road to fulfilling our purpose is a continuum. That through every experience (good or bad) there are many other purposes that we are fulfilling along the way. Clearly stated, I believe that while we are being prepared, shaped, and defined on this predetermined road through life's experiences such as love and relationships, we are also fulfilling intermediate purposes that lead us to our ultimate purpose in life. Our ultimate purpose is the sum total of all that we are to accomplish in life, intermediate pitfalls and poor decisions, although frustrating, are a part of the process.

Each level of maturity is determined by how well we learn from the events we encounter in life (cause and effect). Events are experiences we live out in life. They are divinely prearranged to fit a certain cause God has determined necessary for where and what He have prepared for us. It is when one understands that there is a reason for the pitfalls that the path is easier to travel. This understanding will bring ease to the frustration of the journey, an answer to the uncertainty of the unseen, and clarity to the mystery that continues to unfold in life.

Then comes our ability to accept that everything we encounter in life is simply a part of the perfecting process of life itself. It is one thing to know that it is a part of the process, yet it is another thing to accept it. We must get to the place where we accept that this process is preparation for maximum living and our effective functioning in this world. Like it or not, it is a God-truth and there is no getting around it. The sooner we discover and begin to internalize this truth, the sooner we can begin to reassess life's experiences and begin to add value and meaning to what we have gone through.

Positioning Yourself for God's Blessings and Prosperity

It was amazing to see how God would intersect William's life with the individuals that were critical for his success and for the next chapter in his life. Imagine where William would be at this point of his story if he chose to lament over his losses and accept harmful information about his future. Let us go a step further. What if William wasn't in the educational, spiritual, and physical place at the appointed time when his path crossed with Bishop Potter or Chancellor Colson? All of the opportunities that we have seen come into William life would not have been possible. It would be like God placing you in this world to be a certified public accountant so that you could impact a certain corporate environment, but you never push yourself to complete college. Then one day, when it was His appointed time to intersect your life with the person and the opportunity, you were not qualified to be considered for the position. The larger picture of William's story is that God was orchestrating every single detail to its completion, but William needed to be properly prepared and properly positioned.

Let me state it this way, William's responsibility within God plan was to prepare for his future, to listen and obey God's direction, to walk through the current open doors, to work with integrity and passion wherever God led him, and to trust God for the results and the next open door. In essence, where God was taking William was already predetermined. How he would get there existed within the parameters of God's written plan for William's life.

Personal empowerment and spiritual development is critical if we are to position ourselves for the blessing and prosperity God desires for us. Although there have been some not so Godly teachings on prosperity, I do believe in the principle of prosperity. To me, prosperity is the residual effect of the perfecting process experienced in the seasonal changes in life. I further contend that prosperity is much more than the acquisition of assets, liquid or tangible. It is a much deeper valuation of self. For this reason, assets should not be the consuming focus in your life, nor should it be an issue of constant concern; it should just *be* as a result of your earnest pursuit of knowing and fulfilling your purpose.

In Matthew 6:33, Christ declares, "But seek ye first the kingdom of God and His righteousness, and all of these things will be added unto you." Therefore, our objective in life should be to pursue that which is considered the proper perspective (that which is right in the eyes of God, our source). This will allow the prosperity that has already been predetermined and assigned to our journey in life, to be released in our lives at the time and place intended.

> Behind the curtain of cause is purpose—it is the reason why someone is born, or why something happens.

King Solomon wrote, "To everything there is a season, and a time to every purpose under the heaven" (Ecclesiastes 3:1). By divine authorization, this wise king was sharing with the world a principle for understanding the mystery of life's eventful journey. This principle affirms that the divine plan of life consists of these two facts: (1) everything we experience in life has been assigned to specific seasons, (2) like the natural seasons of the earth, they are timed to fulfill a specific purpose on the road of destiny. In reality, nothing is by chance. Everything has a purpose. Whatever you're experiencing in life, whether negative or positive, it is for your good. Therefore, know that the season you're experiencing this very moment will not last forever; it is on a divine timer that is due to expire at the point of achieving its assigned purpose.

Another Face of Cause and Effect

At the beginning of this chapter we took a look at cause and effect in reference to the relationship between actions and events such that one or more are the result of the other or others. Simply stated, a cause is *why* something happens, and the effect is *what* happens. Behind the curtain of cause is purpose—the reason why something needs to happen.

As we close Chapter 14, we shall look at another face of cause and effect. In its generic scientific term, it is the law of attraction, which is also known in the Bible as the law of sowing and reaping. It is a universal law. Like all universal laws, the law of sowing and reaping is extremely important to grasp if you are to learn to attract the blessings and favor of God that you desire into your life.

Like all other universal laws that have been put into place by God, the law of cause and effect is unchanging, unwavering, deliberate, and precise in its application and delivery. It, like all of the other universal laws, knows no prejudice and delivers in exact proportion the same to all, regardless of belief, age, gender, origin, or religion based on the seeds that you choose to plant.

Think of your experiences as the fruit of a seed you have sown. You can trace every experience you have ever had back a one single seed of choice or decision. A seed-decision was sown in the ground of a moment in your life and in time or in its season, the fruit of that moment came into fruition. Hence the very familiar biblical principles, "Do not be deceived, God is not mocked; for whatever a man sows, that he will also reap" (Galatians 6:7, NKJV). The other says, "But this I say: He who sows sparingly will also reap sparingly, and he who sows bountifully will also reap bountifully" (2 Corinthians 9:6, NKJV). The first reference speaks to your deeds—what you put in. On the other hand, the second reference speaks to your proportion—how much you put in.

The key person of interest in this principle is YOU. What are you sowing as it relates to your future in the area of education, career, relationships, finances, and your spiritual life? How much of your self—your passion are you investing in your future aspirations? Keep in mind, whatever you put in is what you can expect to return back to you when it is time. Every choice has a consequence. If we make wise, Godly decisions, we can expect God to reward us for our consistent trust in Him and His word. If we make impulsive or corrupt choices, we can anticipate negative consequences.

Both verses describe an unalterable law that affects everyone in all areas of life—family, work, finances, and pleasure. It is both

190

a warning and an encouragement. Unlike man made laws, it is inescapable and delivers back to you the results of whatever you give within the parameters of your life experiences and opportunities. This is dependent on whatever action or inaction you choose to take—or not take.

Our return in life is always in proportion to whatever we have given of ourselves. For example, the student who invest time in study and preparation will get the pleasure and satisfaction of valuable knowledge which sharpens his intellectual acumen. This student cannot stay hidden behind closed doors, but rather in the world he's been chosen to make impact on, the door of life will open for him. He will never need to hold his head down in shame, but he will have the courage to face the challenges which confront us all in life. The opposite is true for the student who approaches his preparation for life with a lackadaisical attitude and a minimalist effort that pleads for passion.

> Every choice has a ripple effect of consequences.

A robust faith is required to comprehend and accept the purpose behind the curtain of cause. A tenacious desire to succeed is necessary to firmly grasp the principles that are critical for purpose to be fulfilled, yet we know how seldom such thoughts enter our mind. We habitually stand in our situations in life and look back by faith to see the past filled with God and His plans. We look forward and see Him inhabiting our future; but our now is uninhabited except for ourselves. This is because we fail to invite Him to participate in our affairs fearing He may not want what we desire or perhaps He may not agree with decisions we want to make.

In the eternal scheme of things, we are not so eager to search for truth—to know and see what God has in store for us behind the curtain of cause. In fact, it is not we who are pursuing after God. It is God calling after us! If it were not for God's concern for us, His desire to make known the amazing life we can have in Him, and the unfathomable purpose He has planned for us, we would be forever forsaken. God relentlessly pursues man because He knows He is our greatest need. Even though we rebel against Him and pursue our own sin-filled interests, His quest continues. *While you were doing all these things, declares the Lord, I spoke to you again and again, but you did not listen; I called you, but you did not answer* (Jeremiah 7:13, paraphrased). What an astonishing thought! Behind the curtain of cause—eternal purpose, heaven's splendor: Almighty God is in pursuit of you and me.

ABOUT THE AUTHOR

Dr. Preston Williams II is the author of four books: *By the Way* (2000), *Whispering Silhouette* (2006), *Necessary Changes* (2009), and *The God of How* (2013). In the early 1990s, Dr. Williams was the familiar radio host of "Soul to Soul" and cohost of the Christian TV talk show "Celebrate!" in Savannah, Georgia. His charismatic personality allows him to walk seemingly between two contradictory worlds: religious/secular, African American/Non-African American, and young/old.

Known for his engaging lectures and motivational empowerment sessions, Dr. Williams has traveled nationally as well as internationally for over thirty-nine years speaking to churches, colleges, civic organizations, and businesses. He is known among his peers as a thought-provoking speaker, educator, prolific author, and poet. He addresses critical issues affecting every aspect of human, social, and spiritual development.

Dr. Williams's educational development included undergraduate studies at Howard University, Lee University, and graduate studies at Logos University. He holds several degrees including a BA in theology, an MA in theological studies, and a PhD in psychology and Christian counseling. In 2018, he was awarded a Doctor of Divinity degree from Aidan University. He is a certified behavioral therapist with advanced certification in Christian counseling. He is an ordained bishop and a distinguished member of the American Association of Christian Counselors. Dr. Williams currently serves as Senior Pastor of Gateway Church in Fort Lauderdale, Florida.

He also serves as its senior vice president, and he was recently elected Chairman of the Board of Regents for Logos University, headquartered in Jacksonville, Florida.

The son of a Pentecostal preacher/pastor, Dr. Williams grew up in a small town in southeast Georgia, where he was surrounded by the simple philosophies of family, community, education, and religion. These complementary perspectives served as inspiration for his unique ability to challenge, engage, and enlighten audiences with a message of personal empowerment and spiritual growth.

He and his wife, Kathy, are committed to the ministry of education and personal empowerment for the world. They are the proud parents of six children: Shantal, Preston III, Portia, Jarell, Sharmayne, and Zaynah.

ENDNOTES

Prologue

[1] Daniel C. Rhodes, *Navigating Life with God's Compass* (Decatur, GA: Destiny Navigators, LLC, 2012), 2.

Chapter 1

[1] Tosin Adeola, *Thinking Like God* (Charleston: Createspace, 2016). 52

Chapter 2

[1] PTJ:RS, 9:340-41. Transcription available at Founders Online.

[2] John Bevere, *The Bait of Satan: Living Free from the Deadly Trap of Offense* (Lake Mary, FL: Charisma House, 2014), 7.

Chapter 3

[1] Leslie D. Weatherhead, *The Will of God* (Nashville, TN: Abingdon Press, 1972), Loc. 578 Kindle Book.

Chapter 4

[1] Tom Stella, *The God Instinct: Heeding Your Heart's Unrest* (Notre Dame, IN: Sorin Books, 2001), 155.

Chapter 5

1 Brennan Manning, *Abba's Child: The Cry of the Heart for Intimate Belonging* (Colorado Springs, CO, NavPress, 2015), 24. Kindle.

2 James Finley, *Merton's Place of Nowhere* (Notre Dame, IN, Ave Maria Press, 1978), 9.

3 Robert Sokolowski, *Eucharistic Presence: A Study in the Theology of Disclosure* (Washington, DC: The Catholic University of America Press, 1994), 9.

Chapter 6

1 Max Lucado, *More to Your Story: Discover Your Place in God's Plan* (Nashville, TN, Thomas Nelson, 2016), 22.

2 Denise Wynn, *When God Says No: Finding the Faith to Accept God's Will* (Lantern Books, 2001), e-book Loc. 307 Kindle Book.

Chapter 7

1 C.S. Lewis, *Mere Christianity* (New York, NY: HarperOne Publisher, 2009), 123-4.

Chapter 8

1 Collin Hansen, *Our Secular Age: Ten Years of Reading and Applying Charles Taylor* (Nashville, TN: The Gospel Coalition, 2017), 5.

2 Tony Evans, *Returning to Your First Love* (Chicago, IL: Moody Publishers, 1995), 92.

Chapter 9

1 Harold D. Fishbein, *Peer Prejudice and Discrimination: The Origin of Prejudice* (Mahwah, NJ: Lawrence Erlbaum Associates, Inc., 2010), 2-3.

[2] Dennis McCallum, *The Death of Truth: Responding to Multiculturalism, the Rejection of Reason and the New Postmodern Diversity* (Minneapolis, MN: Bethany House Publishers, 1996), 158.

Chapter 10

[1] Steve Timmis, *I Wish Jesus Hadn't Said That: Finding Joy in the Inconvenience of Discipleship* (Grand Rapids, MI: Zondervan, 2014), 7-8.

Chapter 11

[1] Armand M. Nicholi, Jr., *The Question of God* (New York, NY: Free Press, 2002), 243.

Chapter 12

[1] Friedrich Nietzsche, *Beyond Good and Evil* (London, England: Penguin Group, 1973), 57.

Chapter 13

[1] H. Newton Malony, *The Psychology of Religion for Ministry* (Mahwah, NJ: Paulist Press, 1995), 95-96.

Chapter 14

[1] Richard H. Cox, *The Sacrament of Psychology* (Sanford, FL: InSync Press, 2002), 95.

[2] James K. A. Smith, *How (not) to Be Secular: Reading Charles Taylor.* Print.

Chapter 15

[1] Eric Fellman, *The Power Behind Positive Thinking: Unlocking Your Spiritual Potential* (New York, NY: HarperCollins Publishers, 1996), 23.

Chapter 16

[1] J.I. Packer, *Knowing Christianity* (Downers Grove, IL: InterVarsity Press, 1995), 9-10.

[2] Joel S. Goldsmith, *Practicing the Presence* (New York, NY: HarperCollins Publishers, 1986), 25.

Chapter 17

[1] William Hines, *Leaving Yesterday Behind* (Fearn, Ross-shire, Great Britain: Christian Focus Publications, 2002), 146.

BIBLIOGRAPHY

1. Adeola, Tosin. *Thinking Like God.* Charleston, SC: Createspace, 2016.
2. Bevere, John. *The Bait of Satan: Living Free from the Deadly Trap of Offense.* Lake Mary, FL: Charisma House, 2014.
3. Cox, Richard H. *The Sacrament of Psychology.* Sanford, FL: InSync Press, 2002.
4. Evans, Tony. *Returning to Your First Love.* Chicago, IL: Moody Publishers, 1995.
5. Fellman, Eric. *The Power Behind Positive Thinking: Unlocking Your Spiritual Potential.* New York, NY: HarperCollins Publishers, 1996.
6. Finley, James. *Merton's Place of Nowhere* (Notre Dame, IN, Ave Maria Press, 1978), 9.
7. Fishbein, Harold D. *Peer Prejudice and Discrimination: The Origin of Prejudice.* Mahwah, NJ: Lawrence Erlbaum Associates, Inc. 2010.
8. Goldsmith, Joel S. *Practicing the Presence.* New York, NY: Harper Collins Publishers, 1986.
9. Hansen, Collin and Derek Rishmawy. *Our Secular Age: Ten Years of Reading and Applying Charles Taylor.* Nashville, TN: The Gospel Coalition, 2017.
10. Hines, William. *Leaving Yesterday Behind.* Fearn, Ross-shire, Great Britain: Christian Focus Publications, 2002.
11. Lanahan, Daniel. *When God Says No.* New York, NY: Lantern Books, 2001.

12. Lewis, C. S. *Mere Christianity*. New York, NY: HarperOne Publisher, 2009.

13. Lucado, Max. *More to Your Story: Discover Your Place in God's Plan*. Nashville, TN: Thomas Nelson, 2016.

14. Maloney, H. Newton. *The Psychology of Religion for Ministry*. Mahwah, NJ: Paulist Press, 1995.

15. Manning, Brennan. *Abba's Child: The Cry of the Heart for Intimate Belonging*. Colorado Springs, CO: NavPress, 2015.

16. McCallum, Dennis. *The Death of Truth: Responding to Multiculturalism, the Rejection of Reason and the New Postmodern Diversity*. Minneapolis, MN: Bethany House Publishers, 1996.

17. Nicholi, Jr., Armand M. *The Question of God*. New York, NY: Free Press, 2002.

18. Nietzsche, Friedrich. *Beyond Good and Evil*. London, England: Penguin Group, 1973.

19. PTJ:RS, 9:340-41. Transcription available at Founders Online.

20. Packer, J. I. *Knowing Christianity*. Downers Grove, IL: InterVarsity Press, 1995.

21. Rhodes, Daniel C. *Navigating Life with God's Compass*. Decatur, GA: Destiny Navigators, LLC, 2012.

22. Smith, James K. A. *How (not) to Be Secular: Reading Charles Taylor*. Print.

23. Sokolowski, Robert. *Eucharistic Presence: A Study in the Theology of Disclosure*. Washington, DC: The Catholic University of America Press, 1994.

24. Stella, Tom. *The God Instinct: Heeding Your Heart's Unrest*. Notre Dame, IN: Sorin Books, 2001.

25. Timmis, Steve. *I Wish Jesus Hadn't Said That: Finding Joy in the Inconvenience of Discipleship*. Grand Rapids, MI: Zondervan, 2014.

26. Weatherhead, Leslie D. *The Will of God*. Nashville, TN: Abingdon Press, 1972.

27. Wynn, Denise. *When God Says No*. Lantern Books, 2001.

INDEXING

cognitive 2, 3, 5

commitment xi, xvi, 3, 51, 75, 97, 146

competitiveness 38

complacency 103

compulsivity 81

conflict vi, xiii, xv, xix, xx, xxi, xxiv,
    xxvii, 7, 10, 11, 14, 15, 16, 17,
    18, 19, 20, 21, 22, 23, 25, 30,
    40, 42, 57, 70, 76, 81, 82, 108,
    112, 140, 144, 177, 186

conformity 8, 30

confrontation 14, 15, 16, 17, 19, 20,
    21, 23, 25, 36, 209

Confucius xxi

conscious xix, 37, 41, 81, 126

consecration xxiii

consensus 8

consequence xxiv, 26, 27, 32, 33,
    34, 71, 72, 84, 112, 164, 180,
    190, 191

conviction 19, 23, 50, 51, 98, 145, 186

corruption 10

C. S. Lewis 71, 112, 143

cycle 6, 7, 21, 22, 53

D

David 34, 35, 41, 59, 60, 61, 62, 69,
    93, 107, 135, 165, 166, 171, 172

decision xvi, xix, xxi, xxii, xxiii, xxiv,
    3, 4, 5, 7, 8, 10, 11, 12, 13, 15,
    26, 27, 28, 29, 30, 31, 32, 33,
    34, 35, 37, 67, 75, 80, 110, 121,
    144, 145, 146, 147, 164, 167,
    179, 187, 190, 191

defiance 71, 72, 144

deficiencies 130

degenerative 10

delusion 82, 135

desensitized 18

destination xiv, 110, 154

deterrent 129

dialogue 1, 3, 59

Dietrich Bonhoeffer 94

dimension 11, 27, 136

discourage 14

E

emotion xix, 2, 3, 4, 5, 6, 7, 8, 28, 37,
    40, 41, 46, 54, 88, 149, 177

emotional 2, 3, 4, 6, 7, 8, 21, 38, 39,
    42, 54, 60, 80, 85, 103, 125,
    127, 147, 158, 159, 160

euro-centric 120

existential 158, 159

F

fallen world xx, xxi, 37, 38

fallible 12, 20, 52, 179

false gods 82

finisher xv

free choice 144

free will 57, 143, 144, 151, 182

Friedrich Nietzsche 114, 197

fruition xv, 190

G

glorify 23, 131, 132

goals 3, 12, 21, 27, 53, 105, 110, 118,
    126, 133, 164

God-honoring 21

God-identity 116, 117

Gordon Allport 86

gratification 28, 78

Great Commission 133

greed 8, 87

H

heart-thinking 1, 2, 5, 6, 7, 8, 10, 11,
    12, 13, 108

Helen Keller 58

Hinduism xxi

By the same author:

By the Way:
A Snapshot Diagnosis of the Inner-city Dilemma.
By the Way takes us beyond the theoretical and hypothetical to
the hands-on and feet-on-the-street knowledge of the inner city.
Few have written as pointedly on the subject of the inner city
and its need for true renewal through a confrontation with the
Gospel and the power of the Holy Spirit to change lives, homes,
communities, and then cities and regions that are at risk.

Whispering Silhouette:
The Diary of a Reluctant Poet Giving a Voice to His
Thoughts on Life, Love, and Relationships
The poetry of *Whispering Silhouette* involves not only examining
life, but also taking an honest look at the delicate matrix of love.
It was not written to be a manual of truth, it is a poetic book of
experiences, observations, and random personal thoughts that
chronicle the life of the author over a period of twenty-seven years.

Necessary Changes:
A Guide Through the Four Seasons of Life
Necessary Changes is about personal and spiritual life management.
It is a manual of understanding why you are going through what
you're going through at this time in your life. It is about your
relationship with yourself, your friends, your loved ones, and the
choices you must make at different points during your journey
toward becoming the best you there can be. It is about changing
those things in your life that can be changed and accepting
those you cannot change and trusting God with everything.

The God of How:
Understanding How Trials, Transitions, and
Triumphs Fit into God's Plan for Your Life
The God of How is a captivating book of understanding God's involvement in life's many transitions. It gives insight as to why you are going through what you're going through at this time in your life. It deals with your relationship with yourself, your friends, your loved ones, and the choices you must make at different points during your quest toward becoming the best you there can be. It is a bedrock of wisdom about following one's own path.

For further information on speaking engagements,
seminars, his current US itinerary, and to buy
copies of this book in bulk, please contact:
Preston Williams II Ministries, Inc.
(A nonprofit organization)
Webpage: drpw2inc.org
Email: DrPrestonWilliamsii@drpw2inc.org

Printed in the United States
By Bookmasters